This Must Be Hell

This Must Be Hell

A Look at Pathological Gambling

Hale Humphrey

Writers Club Press
San Jose New York Lincoln Shanghai

Writers Club Press
an imprint of iUniverse, Inc.

For information address:
iUniverse, Inc.
5220 S. 16th St., Suite 200
Lincoln, NE 68512
www.iuniverse.com

ISBN: 0-595-13498-X

Printed in the United States of America

Contents

Introduction

Gambling is pervasive. How many people can say that they have never gambled, never purchased a lottery ticket, played bingo, cards, or bet on their golf games? According to the National Council on Problem Gambling, revenues from legal wagering in the United States have grown by nearly 1,500%. By 1995, the amount wagered legally in the United States had reached $550 billion, or 9% of United States personal income. An individual can make a legal wager in every state except Utah and Hawaii. There are over 700 casinos in operation in twenty-eight states (January 1997).

Once gambling was perceived as a weakness or as sinful. However, gambling is now recognized as a disease. The main features of this disease are that the pathological gambler is emotionally dependent, having lost control over the impulse to gamble. The behavior interferes with normal activities and usually destroys their personal lives. The DSM-IV (Diagnostic and Statistical Manual of Mental Disorders, 4th Edition) categorizes pathological gambling as an Impulse Control Disorder (American Psychiatric Association, 1994).

Not everyone is a compulsive gambler, however. Many may gamble recreationally, spending money as they would on an evening of entertainment. Others are professional gamblers, wagering with cool calculation. But there is no calm connected to the pathological gambler. This individual is as out of control as a toboggan going downhill without a rider. It is a descent into their own person hell.

This book will provide insight into problem gambling, the risks, resources, and recovery. While it can be used as a resource for the professional counselor, or as a text for the student of gambling behavior, *This Must Be Hell* is written in an easy-to-read, non-technical manner for use by the general public.

Part I

WHEN? When does gambling become a problem?

Section I provides a brief overview of gambling, and methods of identifying when gambling becomes problematic.

THIS MUST BE HELL:
An overview of pathological gambling

Jack couldn't stop shivering. It had to be at least 90 degrees in the cell, but he shook as though he were freezing. Continuing to pace the few square feet, he was grateful for the temporary absence of his latest celly. He had a visitor. How could this have happened to him? He asked himself the question for the thousandth time. How would he face everyone? His family? His friends? The shaking worsened.

He'd only borrowed the money from the company. He'd always planned to put it back. The losses kept getting worse. He'd had to increase the bets to get back the original investment. After a while, he just lost count. Then, he forgot about paying it back. He only wanted to keep betting. He wasn't a criminal. He kept repeating the line to himself over and over like a litany. He'd just borrowed the money. Oh, God, he sobbed.

Looking down at his shoes, Jack was reminded that they'd taken his laces. At the time he'd thought it a foolish gesture. Who would kill themselves with their shoelaces? But now, now he searched the small space for a way to end the pain, the humiliation. Every time he thought of facing his wife....

The door clanged open and his cellmate returned. This only happened in movies, Jack thought. The man glaring at him was frightening. His size and strength were only a small part of what made him fearful. The rage that simmered up out of him like toxic fumes was what Jack feared the most. The hatred was so intense that the man needed no small excuse to vent his wrath, taking pleasure in inflicting pain.

This must be hell, Jack thought. There can be nothing worse than this!

Jack had reached what Gambler's Anonymous called *low bottom*. Low bottom was when a gambler has gone as low as he can get. He has lost everything, faces prison, has nothing left. Jack had definitely reached low bottom.

Jack had begun gambling in college, betting on sports events, shooting pool. He always did well. He actually managed to fund his last year of college with his gambling. Losing was never a concern. On the few occasions when Jack did lose, he always made it up on the next bet. Life was good.

As a marketing major and a man who liked action, Jack was drawn to sales. He was a natural. The freedom, the constant travel, and the camaraderie with the other account executives, Jack loved it all. Football season crackled with excitement. Viewed by his colleagues as an expert on picking the right teams, Jack laughed at the guys who spent thousands on services that picked the teams for you. That would take all the fun out of it.

Sometimes one of the guys would get in too deep, losing frequently. They borrowed money from everyone. Then they would get edgy, blowing up. Sometimes they lost their jobs. That would never happen to me, Jack thought. He was riding high.

Jack had been in a winning phase for a long time. According to Dr. Robert L. Custer (1985), there are three phases of gambling. During the winning phase there is excitement and promise. The gambler becomes convinced that he is smarter and luckier than others.

During the losing phase, however, the chase is on. Continued gambling brings increasing losses and borrowing money. Urgency becomes so intense that the gambler may engage in illegal activities. After many years of being in a winning phase, Jack eventually began to lose. At first he wasn't worried. He would just win it back. Then the losses started to get bigger. It was too embarrassing to borrow money from the other guys. He had to keep up the pretense that he was on top. He started taking out extra credit cards, and taking out large cash advances. He took a loan out on his home. He told his wife it was to invest in stock. He removed the money put aside for their children's college fund. Before long his available

Jack started padding his expenses, but that wasn't nearly enough. Soon he began taking small amounts from company accounts. He was certain he could return it. Somehow, in the beginning, miraculously, it wasn't missed. The amount grew. Shortly before he was arrested, Jack entered the desperation phase of his gambling.

The desperation phase, according to Custer, is the end of the line. The gambler experiences a form of panic when he runs out of options. During this phase, gamblers may engage in illegal or unethical activities, acts that they would never have believed themselves capable. Many gamblers reach the desperation phase several times before they hit their low bottom. Jack was in a constant panic by this point. He had lost track of his juggling and went from one bet to another, thinking each bet would be the solution to his problems. By this time, he had no idea how much money he truly needed to pull out of the riptide in which he'd found himself.

For Jack, the main source of the panic was the fear of discovery. Incarceration was not a reality, but to be revealed as anything but a winner was unacceptable. Jack's wife knew he bet on sports, and that he was very intense when he watched the games, but she was totally unaware of the extent of his gambling activities. To his two kids, Jack was a hero, a funny guy who brought home presents. Sometimes, especially lately, he was unpredictable. Once, when his son was trying to get his attention during the final moments of a game, Jack slapped him with the back of his hand.

When Jack's wife was informed of Jack's incarceration she was shocked and confused. At first, she was convinced that it was a mistake. Since Jack had always managed the funds, she had little knowledge of their financial situation. When she went through his papers, to see how much she could raise for bail, her shock and confusion turned to rage. Although she was naturally upset about what Jack had done to their financial situation, the major source of her rage was that she felt betrayed. He had lied to her. The betrayal was no less than if he had been having an affair. Jack would never understand why she was so angry. He believed that she was disillusioned because he wasn't the winner he claimed to be.

Jack had lost touch with reality. The Gamblers Anonymous 'COMBO' book describes the world of the compulsive gambler as a dream world in which a lot of time is spent creating images of the great and wonderful things they are going to do as soon as they make the big win. When they win, they gamble to dream still greater dreams. But when failing, they gamble in reckless desperation and the depths of their misery are fathomless as their dream world comes crashing down. Sadly, they will struggle back, dream more dreams and suffer more misery. No one can convince them that their great schemes will not some day come true. They believe they will, for without this dream world, life would be intolerable.

Jack is an example of an action gambler. According to Lesieur (1993) action relates to the thrill-seeking, risk-taking way of life. The state of arousal produced by gambling becomes as addictive as a drug. Characteristics associated with an action gambler include a need for high achievement, exhibitionism, dominance, and endurance.

Jack came from a caring and loving family. He was not abused nor neglected. Jack had not been especially good in school, his grades were average, but he excelled in sports and was very popular. Jacks parents were proud of his accomplishments. At an early age, Jack learned to enjoy the privileges of success. He minimized his flaws, lying to cover up mistakes so that his parents would not be disappointed. While they never indicated to Jack that they would love him less if he were not socially and athletically successful, he internalized that belief, needing to maintain his image at all costs. When he married, he chose a wife who idolized him and bought into his image without question. He never conveyed to her any feelings, no matter how small, of insecurity or fear. He always managed to provide more than she requested. If she wanted a cloth coat, she got a fur. Everything was always the best. She never questioned his ability to provide these things. She learned early in their relationship that Jack did not bode well with challenges to his authority. The charm and charisma of the action gambler is hard to resist, and it becomes easy for the spouse to enter into collaboration to perpetuate the image of perfection.

Not all compulsive gamblers are action gamblers, however. Unlike Jack, some are attracted to a more passive form of gambling, or luck gambling, such as slot machines. They are referred to as escape gamblers. The escape gambler seeks to escape from stress or loneliness by entering into a self-hypnotic state. While slot playing is a solitary activity, people, lights, and noise surround the player. There is an overall sense of acceptance. One may wander about the casino without feelings of self-consciousness. Sometimes there is an emotional attachment to the machine, and players will resist leaving it. They may stay with the machine for hours, often to the point of incontinence, ignoring other basic biological drives such as hunger and thirst.

Mary is one example of an escape gambler. Mary began going to the casinos with a group of friends as recreation. The first time she went she won $3,000. She was ecstatic. She didn't go back for several months, but the second time she won again, this time $1,000. She'd never felt this good before. Sometimes the stress and pressures of her job and family seemed overwhelming. There was never any time that was her own. When she was at the casino, however, she felt free, relaxed. She began stopping off at the casino on her way home from work. She'd always arrived home an hour or two before everyone else, so it was her time. She'd spend about 45 minutes at the casino and manage to arrive home in time to be with her family. They didn't know where she'd been.

One evening, she'd lost a lot of money and was feeling panicky. She felt she needed to get it back. For the first time, she took her credit card to the ATM machine and got cash. She lost track of time. When she arrived home, she was two hours late and her family was in a panic.

She felt so guilty she admitted to them that she had been going to the casino, and swore that she would stop. They seemed surprised, but happy that she was all right, and satisfied that she had it under control.

Mary stayed away from he casino for three weeks. One day she had a bad headache and left work early. She'd planned to go home, take a pill, and go to bed. Instead she found herself driving to the casino. Well, she thought, it had been a long time. I deserve it. She soon forgot her headache.

Mary managed to leave the casino in time to get home before her family. She began leaving work just a little early so that she could stop off for "just one hour." She even bought a watch with an alarm and set it so that she would remember to leave in time.

Mary continued her routine until one night when she began to win a lot. She turned off her watch and continued playing. She was really hot that night. She left the casino with $2,000.

When she arrived home, her family were subdued. She was excited and showed them the money she won. They were not as thrilled. Her son looked at her in a manner that she had never seen before, a look of disgust.

After dinner, Mary's sister and her husband came to the house. They talked to her about her gambling problem, suggesting that she go to Gambler's Anonymous.

"But I don't have a problem," she protested. "The casinos are full of people. You think they are all compulsive gamblers?"

Mary reluctantly agreed to attend Gambler's Anonymous. She went to one meeting. The room was filled primarily with men who talked loud and smoked constantly. They had voted on the smoking issue she was told. Did she have any objections? She looked around the room and decided that she had no objections.

Mary didn't seem to have anything in common with these gamblers. They gambled on anything and everything. They seemed to take pride in the huge amounts of money they had lost in one night. When Mary left the meeting she was convinced of one thing. If this was what compulsive gambling looked like, then she must not be a compulsive gambler.

Mary learned to be more careful about her time at the casino. She took out credit cards in her name only, using her work address, so that her husband wouldn't know about the cash advances. When she couldn't pay the cards, she sent in the minimum. Her family just didn't understand.

One evening Mary was running late. She drove toward the casino, knowing that her family would be waiting for her at home, and she knew when she didn't arrive soon they would be disappointed. Yet she couldn't bring herself to turn the car around. The closer she got the more she despised herself. Still she couldn't stop. She had to be there.

The moment she entered the casino she felt at peace. She was suddenly calm. She didn't care about her family. She took out a $100 bill and inserted it into the machine. This is all the cash I have, she told herself. When this is gone, I will have to leave. I have no choice. She began to play the $1 machine. It was good to her tonight. She hit twice for $50.00. This was going to be her night. Putting three coins at a time into the machine, she was convinced this was the only way to make any money. Her coin buckets were full. She had over $400. Time to stop.

What about the $10,000 you owe, a voice inside of her asked. You're hot tonight. You could get it all. Then you could quit for good. She began feeding the machine again, three coins at a time. An hour later, the buckets were empty. She reached inside for another handful of coins. Nothing. It was all gone.

"Would you watch my seat?" she asked the man beside her. He nodded absently.

Mary walked the few feet to the ATM machine and entered her credit card. It was declined. She ran through three more before she finally got one that gave her money.

Mary won another $300 that night, and gave it back. She couldn't get any more cash from her cards.

She walked back to her car in a daze. What have I done? she asked herself. She could see the faces of her husband and son when she walked in the door. They would know where she'd been. How was she going to tell them that she'd taken loans out on the house? The third notice came today. They were going to lose their home.

Mary couldn't face her family. She went to a motel where she counted out thirty pills. She sat for over an hour staring at them.

In her other hand, Mary held a losing lottery ticket. She continued to stare at the 800 number at the bottom of the ticket. "If you, or someone you love, has a gambling problem, call the Gambling Helpline." The sentence was followed by the 800 number. Mary put the pills beside her on the bed and picked up the phone. "I think I need help," she said to the voice on the other end of the line. Mary had reached low bottom.

Many gamblers are driven to the point of desperation and suicide when they realize what they have done to their lives. They see no hope, no way out of the hell surrounding them.

There is still another growing group of problem gamblers, the elderly. They are drawn by loneliness and emptiness. They often begin by taking senior citizen trips to the casinos in buses. Sometimes they wander into the casinos in the daytime as an alternative to walking the malls. In our society, the elderly are scorned or ignored. Their participation is seldom encouraged. The casinos welcome them. They provide inexpensive buffets, free transportation, and allow them to stay as long as they wish. The slot machine becomes their only friend, the casino a haven from the solitude of their lonely homes. They are shocked to discover how quickly they can lose their life savings, hoping each time to win back the money they lost. They are faced with destitution, poverty, and despair.

Many compulsive gamblers began their addiction as children, playing card games with relatives, going to the races with Dad or Uncle Joe. Some frequented bingo games. After all, the church sanctions bingo. Others state that they never really gambled until....

Adolescents are drawn to gambling as a form of excitement. Sometimes gambling activities provide an avenue for success or belonging. For other adolescents, gambling, like alcohol and drugs, becomes an escape from the many stressors of this difficult developmental stage. Magical thinking, which is the key to the gambling mentality, is also the cornerstone of the teen years. Parents and other adults often sanction the activity as socially acceptable and wholesome entertainment. The seriousness of the problem may not emerge for years.

Gambling has been a socially acceptable activity in America since its earliest days. The American Revolution was partly financed by lottery revenues. In 1811, the Commonwealth of Pennsylvania raised money to construct the Union Canal through lottery revenues (Gordon (1833). Consequently, most perceive gambling as innocent fun.

The addiction can affect anyone. All age groups, income levels, and cultures are affected.

If you think you have a problem with gambling, then you probably do. The best self check for compulsive gambling is the one question: Is this interfering with my life?

Are you spending more money, more time gambling than you can afford? Are you neglecting activities and people that are important to you? Are you beginning to engage in behaviors, such as lying, in which you would not have believed yourself capable in the past?

DO YOU THINK YOU HAVE A GAMBLING PROBLEM?

Gamblers Anonymous developed the following 20 questions*

- Did you ever lose time from work due to gambling?
- Has gambling ever made your home life unhappy?
- Did gambling affect your reputation?
- Have you ever felt remorse after gambling?
- Did you ever gamble to get money with which to pay debts or otherwise solve financial difficulties?
- Did gambling cause a decrease in your ambition or efficiency?
- After losing did you feel you must return as soon as possible and win back your losses?
- After a win did you have a strong urge to return and win more?
- Did you often gamble until your last dollar was gone?
- Did you ever borrow to finance your gambling?
- Have you ever sold anything to finance gambling?
- Were you reluctant to use "gambling money" for normal expenditures?

- Did gambling make you careless of the welfare of yourself and your family?
ᐁ • Did you ever gamble longer than you had planned?
- Have you ever gambled to escape worry or trouble?
- Have you ever committed, or consider committing, an illegal act to finance gambling?
- Did gambling cause you to have difficulty in sleeping?
- Do arguments, disappointments or frustrations create with you an urge to gamble?
- Did you ever have an urge to celebrate any good fortune by a few hours of gambling?
- Have you ever considered self destruction as a result of your gambling?

According to GA, most compulsive gamblers will answer yes to at least seven of these questions._____
Gambler's Anonymous (1984, 1991).

Part II

WHO? Gender and Age Differences

Section II addresses the differences between males and females and among differing age groups. Specifically, we will look at women who gamble, children at risk and senior citizens.

Women Who Gamble

Elizabeth trembled with rage as she drove away from her house. Why did he always have to treat her like a child? He seemed to be made of stone, void of any feelings.

She could hear her therapist now. *Why don't you assert yourself? Tell him how you feel.* Easy for her. She didn't have to live with him. Elizabeth hadn't told her about the gambling. She doubted she would continue with counseling.

The car seemed to know where she wanted to go. Before long, she could see the billboards advertising the casino. A warm, peaceful wave came over her. Soon, she thought, I will be inside. Then everything will be all right. He can't upset me there.

The moment Elizabeth walked into the slot area, she felt wrapped in a loving cocoon. No one criticized her here. Here she was accepted. Loved. She sighed with pleasure and relief as she slid into the seat before her favorite machine. *I love you, Elizabeth.* The machine seemed to blink at her.

For thirty years, Elizabeth had been a good and faithful corporate wife. She had entertained, kept the house, kept her figure, and always kept her composure. Grace beyond all else was valued for a corporate wife. Her husband was retired now and encroaching on her territory. In the past he'd always been too busy to give her advice, and seemed grateful for her support. Now, he was always there, telling her what to do, what to cook. He was taking gourmet-cooking lessons. What next?

She knew he hated it when she gambled. He'd discovered her secret credit card and hit the ceiling. How could she be so stupid? He'd ranted at her.

Naturally, she swore she wouldn't gamble again. For several months, she stayed away from the casino. The pressure just kept building. Keeping up an image was important in her social world. There was no way she could discuss her feelings with her friends. What would they think of her?

Last year, when one of their friends was going through a divorce, all of them had looked at her with such pity. Elizabeth would hate being looked at in that manner. No, this was her secret place. She was safe here. She just needed to win back the money she'd lost. Maybe she could sell some of those stocks her father left her. They were just lying there, after all. John never had to know.

Unfortunately for Elizabeth, John did discover her continued gambling after she had depleted her personal savings. Fearing that their retirement money would follow suit, he transferred all money into his name only. Elizabeth was infuriated and retaliated by taking money wherever she could find it, sometimes signing his name to checks. Her gambling behavior increased. After two years, John filed for divorce.

While there are some women who engage in action gambling, most women are attracted to escape or luck gambling such as slots or bingo. They gamble to escape personal problems or unpleasant situations in their lives. Many are depressed. Did the depression precede the gambling, or is it a result of the shame and humiliation associated with discovery? Many women gamble to self medicate their depression. For a brief period, the escape and excitement provides some relief. Most find, however, that the circumstances associated with the gambling eventually exacerbated the depression.

Research into female gamblers indicates that a large proportion lack problem solving skills (Scannell, et al, 2000). Many women gamblers escape their difficulties through activities or substances—food, alcohol, prescribed medications, spending, sex, or gambling—rather than working through a logical plan for coping with the situation. In addition, they experience a sense of learned helplessness, believing they have no control over their lives. For many, gambling activity provides an illusion of control and total acceptance.

Generally, women progress toward problem gambling three times faster than males. The tendency may have more to do with the slot preference, since slot machines are considered to be the crack cocaine of gambling addiction. While a racetrack gambler or card player may take twenty or more years to reach low bottom, the average for slots players is two years.

The casinos provide a refuge for women without the stigma of being alone. Many women, particularly those over forty, feel uncomfortable in public places without a companion. At any time of the day or evening, a woman may remain as though invisible while at the same time experiencing a sense of social involvement. The best of both worlds.

While women reach the problem level faster than men, they also experience a stronger sense of shame and guilt while still gambling. Their male counterparts are more likely to experience shame or guilt as the result of social or legal sanctions once the gambling has become problematic in their lives.

Males frequently experience an emotional distance, at times referred to as alexithymia (Krystal, 1982). Alexithymia is a difficulty in articulating feelings. Counselors and family members, who ask why males gamble, are often greeted with pat answers that, in truth, have little to do with the underlying cause of the activity. In most cases, they will state that they wanted money, because that appears to be a logical response. Consequently, males are much less likely to seek help than females, and enter counseling or support groups only after developing serious financial, legal, or relational problems. Shame and guilt over neglecting family responsibilities, or embarrassment over financial difficulties, often drives women to seek help.

Nevertheless, women receive less sympathy for their problem than males. The wife of a gambler is more likely to remain in the marriage than the husband of a gambler. Negligence of family by a female is more socially frowned upon than the same negligence perpetrated by a male.

Help, however, is more difficult to find. Women generally report discomfort at male dominated Gamblers Anonymous meetings. Support groups for women are reported as more comfortable, but harder to locate. Also, not all states provide funded counseling for problem gamblers, and insurance companies are less likely to pay for gambling counseling. In addition, most counselors are not trained in gambling counseling.

If you are a woman who fears she may have a gambling problem, call your local helpline posted in the casino. They can tell you how to obtain the help you need, or just talk to you about the problem. If there is no helpline in your area, read the list of Gambling Councils in the appendix at the back of the book.

Children at Risk

Chuck remembers his first experience with gambling as a special day with Dad. Chuck and his dad would go to the racetrack together. It was always their special secret from Mom. Keeping the day a secret made it all that much more exciting. Father and son shared a secret from the rest of the family. Chuck felt very close to his father on those days.

Chuck's dad bought him his own racing form and taught him to handicap the horses. After he made his selection, Dad would make the bet for him, giving him the winnings to keep for his very own. The money was kept in a shoebox in the back of the closet. Chuck would take it out and count it, remembering the excitement of the races that won him the money.

On some days, however, Dad didn't seem as happy. He snapped at Chuck and kept his winnings. Once, he came into Chuck's room and took the shoebox, saying he needed it. Soon afterward, his parents broke up and Chuck didn't get to see his father as often.

Long after Chuck's father died, Chuck felt him there each time he visited the track, remembering the closeness they'd shared. For Chuck, gambling equaled his relationship with his father.

According to the National Council on Problem Gambling, many adults began gambling as children. Most began gambling with their parents, or watched their parents gamble. According to their research, the earlier an individual begins gambling, the more likely they are to experience problems. Youth whose parents gamble have twice the number of problems with the law and twice the rate of attempted suicide (Jacobs, 1998). The National Gambling Impact Study (1999) states that youth with gambling problems also have family, academic and legal problems. Between 9-14%

of youth are classified as at risk for a gambling problem. Gambling is often associated with alcohol, drug use, truancy, low grades, parents who gamble, and illegal activities (NGIS, 1999).

We may believe that our children are protected because underage gambling is illegal in casinos and racetracks. However, adolescents gamble on cards and sporting events as well as games of skill. Eighteen percent of youths between 12-17 admitted to gambling within the past twelve months.

Mike was a senior in high school we he discovered Internet poker. His parents had given him his own computer as a way to improve his grades and research facts for term papers. They never monitored his activity on the computer, and were not concerned about the late nights he spent on the Internet, believing him hard at work on his studies. Mike easily obtained a credit card, and opened a gambling account. When his card maxed out, he obtained another one, which he also ran up to the limit. Soon, in desperation Mike began taking blank checks from his parents' checkbook. He would write checks to himself, cash them, and pay his cards. Naturally, his behavior was discovered and his gambling habit was unveiled. By this time, however, Mike was in debt for twenty thousand dollars. He had no money, and was planning to enter college the following year. His parents bailed him out. Mike was repentant, and took a part-time job to help pay off the cards. When he entered college, however, his gambling resurfaced. Internet gambling was replaced with all-night poker games. Mike flunked out of school his first year.

A study done by the Alcohol, Tobacco, and Other Drug Abuse among Delaware Students Survey, conducted in 1999, indicates that 31% of Delaware eighth graders gambled, and 27% of Delaware 11th graders gambled. They also found that those eight graders who gambled were 70% more likely to drink alcohol, while the 11th graders were 27% more likely to drink alcohol, 50% more likely to use illegal drugs, and almost twice as likely to shoplift and steal money.

One factor, which may put youth at risk in addition to parental role models, is the increasing use of video games. The hypnotic action of a video game closely resembles that of slot machines. Escapist behaviors can easily become a way of coping with stress. Couple this tendency with an absence of parental supervision and increased social stress, and you have increased the risk factor for youth.

What can we do to reduce the risk to our young people? Public awareness is the first prevention. Get as much information as possible. Second, provide supervision. Monitor the number of hours your child spends playing video games or surfing the Internet. Set controls on your computer to inhibit access to certain sites such as chat rooms and Internet gambling. Communicate with your children frequently. Talk to them about such risks. Identify stressors that are affecting your child, and discuss techniques for managing them. Finally, be aware of the example you are setting for your child. Weekly family poker games may seem innocent, but they could very well be sending a message to your child that gambling is a fun and appropriate family activity.

Senior Gamblers

Until she turned 60, Mary had never gambled more than a dollar in her life. A lifelong housewife, her husband had died a few years earlier, leaving Mary restless and lonely. Her children lived in other states and she saw them only on occasional holidays. The friends she and her husband shared engaged in couples entertainment. She was no longer a couple. Good meaning friends continued to invite her to dinner and other activities, but she was a reminder of what they faced in the near future. She stayed by herself.

With her husband's pension, she lived simply, but comfortably. Her small house was paid for, and she had few expenses and a little money in the bank for occasional extras.

Mary's daily entertainment was to walk the mall, and have lunch in the food court. Sometimes, she would go to an afternoon movie. Mary noticed that other seniors spent their days in much the same way. A friendly gentleman in his early seventies sat down and spoke with her on several occasions. They began to meet at the mall regularly.

During the holiday season, the mall became crowded with shoppers. Mary's new friend suggested that they go to the casino nearby and play the slot machines. Mary had never entered a casino, but thought it sounded intriguing. That day, Mary won $2,500 playing quarter slots. She was elated.

Mary's family visited over the holiday, and she didn't see her friend for a few weeks. In January, she returned to the mall. He was waiting for her. It was a cold, miserable day. Why not go to the casino?

There was no winter in the casino. It was always brightly lighted and cheerful. People were friendly and didn't stare at you in sympathy the way they sometimes did at the mall or other public places. On this day, Mary won another $3,000. It was amazing.

Mary's friend developed a bad cold, and didn't show up at the mall for a while. Mary began to go to the casino alone. She was thrilled to find another place where she could wander about without feeling self-conscious. Everyone was so friendly there, and they began sending her little coupons for free parking and buffet discounts.

Mary stopped going to the mall. Each morning, she would dress and go to the casino with twenty dollars to put in the quarter machines. Life had definitely become more interesting.

The first day that Mary lost her twenty dollars without winning she was disappointed. The next day, she lost again. She was becoming angry. This was not as much fun. Mary began taking more money with her each day, but kept losing. After a few weeks, she realized that she had lost several thousand dollars. She began withdrawing money from her bank account.

She knew she had to win again soon, and she did. This time, however, she won $500. She knew she had lost a lot more, however, so she continued to play. They more money she spent, she reasoned, the more likely she was to win. Soon, the winnings were also gone, and Mary had spent another $100 of her own money.

It took less than a year for Mary to empty her precious bank account. Desperate, she took out a home equity loan. She had to win the money back. Soon that money was gone also, and she had no options.

Seniors are drawn to the warmth and comfort of the casinos, where they can roam undisturbed for hours at a time. They escape their loneliness by surrounding themselves with crowds of people, glitter, and noise.

Senior centers offer trips to Atlantic City and other casinos. The trips are inexpensive, at times even free. Not wanting to cook for themselves, they are drawn to the buffets, which are often discounted.

Unlike our young and even middle-aged gamblers, seniors do not have the option of recovering the damage done by gambling. They are usually drawn to slots, which are considered the crack cocaine of gambling. They lose their savings, their homes, and their chance for a comfortable retirement. Families quickly become disgusted and frustrated, not understanding why their older relatives are behaving so badly.

Are some seniors more vulnerable to gambling? McNeilly and Burke (200) looked at some differences between active senior gamblers and non-active senior gamblers. They discovered that active senior gamblers are more likely to smoke, drive a car, eat fewer than two meals a day, and do volunteer work. Non-active senior gamblers spent more time reading books. This research might indicate that non-active gamblers are better able to entertain themselves alone than active senior gamblers who are driven to seek entertainment outside of themselves.

The extended family is a thing of the past. The nuclear family frequently moves away or is too busy to interact with parents and grandparents, and elderly aunts and uncles. Women outlive their spouses, and find themselves alone. Our society abandons and isolates its elderly, leaving them to find social activities and comfort elsewhere. Many of them find it in the casinos.

Part III

WHY? Causes of problem gambling

Section III addresses various causes of problem gambling, including biological factors, trait or personality factors, and gambling as learned behavior.

Biological Factors related to gambling

It is after midnight. Everyone in the house is asleep, except John. The room is dark except for the glow of the computer screen. John stares, fixated into the screen, as he plays game after game of video poker. Each hand is costing him between five and twenty dollars. John gets no more than four hours of sleep per night. He paces restlessly, throughout the day, unable to focus on one activity for more than a few minutes at a time. The only time John can concentrate and relax is when he gambles.

John has been diagnosed with bi-polar disorder, but refuses treatment and/or medication. He is medicating his problem with gambling. His problem is clearly a bio-chemical one, but for many the answer is not so understandable.

Many gamblers suffer from anxiety related disorders. The gambling activity helps to calm them down. For others, gambling provides an anti-depressant that enables them to cope with feelings of hopelessness and sadness. Sometimes the symptoms of depression are the result of the devastation brought on by gambling. Often it is difficult to determine which came first.

The nature/nurture argument continues in an attempt to understand why some people develop a gambling problem and others do not. Why is it that a multitude of individuals can gamble recreationally without devastation? There is increasing evidence to indicate that there are actually differences in the brains of pathological gamblers and non-problem gamblers.

There is much that is not known or understood about how the brain functions. However, with PET (positron emission tomography) and MRI (magnetic resonance imagery) we can obtain images of brain functions.

An MRI is similar to a CAT scan, but passes the subject's head through a magnetic fluid to align the brain's atoms. An MRI can take clear and detailed pictures of the brain's soft tissues.

PET scans measure the amount of glucose burned in a given region, producing an enhanced color picture. Hot colors such as red, orange, and yellow indicate more activity while cool colors such as violet, blue, and green indicate less activity.

Studies done by Pasternak, et. Al. (1999) indicate that gambling activity can actually change the cerebral blood flow in specific peak areas such as the middle frontal gyrus, orbital gyrus, and inferior frontal gyrus. What this means is that during gambling activity we light up or stimulate parts of the brain. Such activity then is similar to consumption of a drug that stimulates the dopamine reward system, giving us a sense of pleasure.

Consequently, if gambling creates activity in the brain, it increases our potential for becoming addicted to, or at the least attracted to, this activity. This still doesn't provide an answer to why some of us? Why not all of us? There are numerous answers to that question. The first is that some of us enter the activity with a predisposition toward addictive behavior.

Rugle and Melamed (1990) for example, state that deficits involving the ability to plan and sequence, to organize and integrate perceptual input, to change perceptual set, and to focus on relevant information actually exist prior to the addiction. Therefore, an individual possessing these deficits is more likely to ignore the inhibitory factors that reduce an activity to a harmless recreation. The logic and reasoning that tells us that we are not likely to win thousands of dollars, or that, having lost our money, it is time to quit, is not present to the same degree in the pathological gambler.

The connectors to different parts of the brain can be inhibited or altered by an increase or decrease in certain neurotransmitters, such as dopamine, seratonin, or acetylcholine. The limbic system is responsible for our emotions, but it must receive information from the temporal lobes and prefrontal cortex. These parts of the brain provide cognitive relevance, processing reality and making appropriate connections for logical reasoning.

Supporting evidence of a predisposition is found by DeObaldie and Parsons (1984), who found a relationship between ADHD (attention deficit hyperactivity disorder) and a later vulnerability to addictive disorders. The inability to focus and concentrate and a need for visual stimulus is a factor in attraction to gambling. In addition, Custer and Custer (1978) state that impulsivity is a predisposition for gambling.

Evidence pointing toward a biological basis for pathological gambling would indicate treatment of the predisposing elements with medication and counseling. Nevertheless, there are other predisposing factors, such as personality and environmental conditioning, which we will discuss in the next two chapters.

Trait and Personality Factors

Jennifer met Vince one year after a very painful divorce. He was charming and attentive and they quickly developed an intense relationship. Jennifer knew that Vince gambled, but she had no indication that his gambling was a problem. Frequently, Jennifer would go with Vince to the track, where he bet on horses. He always kept a journal and, to her knowledge, used only disposable income to gamble. She thought it was cute. A year after their marriage, she discovered that her life savings were depleted and they were over $100,000 in debt with credit cards. Vince had been gambling during the day without her knowledge. When they'd visited the track together, he'd lied about the amount and frequency of his bets. They were forced to declare bankruptcy.

Jennifer was devastated. She felt betrayed and ashamed. She asked Vince to leave. Vince swore that, with help, he could overcome the problem. He was sick.

"Hate the disease, not the diseased," he begged.

Together they attended Gambler's Anonymous and Gamanon, 12-step programs for gamblers and families of gamblers. Jennifer was told she would get over the anger and needed to forgive. She did. They stayed together.

Five years later, Vince was arrested for fraud involving Jennifer's business. He had engaged her clients in phony investment schemes, cheating them out of thousands of dollars. Vince went to jail for twelve years.

Jennifer filed suit for divorce and refused to see Vince again, but her actions were too late. Her business and reputation were destroyed. Few believed that she was not aware of his actions. She came dangerously close to being indicted as a co-conspirator.

Jennifer was not a weak, ineffectual person. She was bright and self-reliant. She had been attracted to Vince's charm and intelligence. He was witty and fun to be with. His lies were extremely convincing. She is not alone. There are many such victims.

Vince was diagnosed with Narcissistic personality disorder. This type of personality disorder is usually charming, bright and highly convincing. His lies appear all the more genuine and believable due to the absence of conscience. One may find themselves easily enmeshed. It is not until their lives are reduced to rubble that they realize what has happened.

The frequency with which we read about such people appears to be increasing. The catastrophic results of the con man's behaviors are no longer something that happens to others. It is becoming more and more important to gain a clearer understanding of this disorder in order to guard against its intrusive devastation.

Anti-social and narcissistic personality disorders are found in a high proportion of gamblers.

The DSM-IV identifies the anti-social personality disorder as an individual who lacks personal loyalties, shows poor judgment and responsibility, and is capable of rationalizing or justifying inappropriate behavior.

The anti-social personality disorder was once referred to as sociopathy or psychopathy. Many professionals feel that the current DSM is not an adequate predictor of the disorder. Meloy (1988) for example states that the antisocial personality disorder as defined in the DSM is too criminally biased and socio-economically skewed. The anti-social personality disorder requires a childhood involvement in criminal or antisocial activities and is a closed-ended checklist which does not allow for subtleties (Harpur, 1994).

A look at life-long con men reveals a similar dilemma. An article published in May, 1996 in The Sun, a Baltimore newspaper, described Michael H. Clott, who had bilked victims out of millions, as having an average childhood.

The difference here is that aggression is not necessarily overt or physical. In 1945, Karen Horney stated that the interpersonal exploitation of others lessens the psychopath's sense of barrenness. This is supported by Kernberg (1975), who views the psychopath as an extreme variant of the narcissistic personality disorder. Kernberg further states that the world of the psychopath is populated by devalued images of self and others.

In 1964, Cleckly wrote about a Mask of Sanity. He believed that the psychopath was merely able to cover, or mask, his psychosis. He further states that the psychopath's lying is so pervasive that some observers have characterized him as unable to tell the truth.

Meloy (1989) fears an increase in psychopathy, and Gardener (1986) states that a lower level of empathy and a higher level of generalized anxiety exists among children who are reared in an image based, multimedia, less attentive society. Our recent acts of violence by children seems to validate his fears.

Most professionals agreed, however, that whether called sociopathy, psychopathy or anti-social personality, there is a certain impulsivity, a lack of guilt, morality, or empathy, and an incapability to form deep or meaningful relationships or learn from experience or punishment.

Another, closely related, personality disorder associated with gambling is the narcissistic personality disorder. The narcissist lacks empathy for others, has a pattern of grandiosity (in fantasy or behavior), and a strong need for admiration. He is interpersonally exploitative, takes advantage of others, believing that he is special and has a sense of entitlement.

Are we, with our emphasis on materialism and artificial stimulation, and our reduction in meaningful human interaction, creating a breeding ground for such personality disorders? How could Jennifer have protected herself against Vince? What were the warning signs that she could have looked for?

For those who love a gambler, it is often a difficult decision to go or stay. After all, he is ill. You wouldn't leave him if he had a physical disorder, would you? He needs you, you say. The decision is ultimately yours.

When tangled in the con man's deceitful web, we are often oblivious to the early warning signs. We find ways to explain them away, or we do not recognize them for the danger signals that they truly are. However, lightening doesn't strike without some warning. Here are some of the signs that the person you are becoming involved with is not what he pretends, and some guidelines to assist you in differentiating between the individual who is suffering from a gambling addiction and the personality disordered, potential con, who also gambles:

Early declarations. When declarations of undying love spew forth after only a few short hours together, you have either found a true soul mate, or, more likely, you are being set up. Love is based on a deeper understanding between two people that usually takes time to develop.

Excitement. Watch for the lure of excitement. Often those very things/people which we find most exciting are tinged with danger; a motorcycle ride, sky diving, bungy jumping. Question exactly what is the attraction to this person. Falling into a relationship with a con man is equivalent to a bungy jump without the bungy.

Inconsistencies. Look for inconsistencies between what he says he believes and what he does. The con may claim to be passionate about some cause or to possess some special talent. He may impress you with his commitment to the environment, but forget to recycle his cans, or he may brag about his artistic abilities, but never paint. Ask for evidence of these claims.

Secrecy. Question frequent, unexplained secrets, including unexplained time lapses and behaviors. Secrecy and guardedness are consistent with the con mentality.

Money. Cons usually like the best of everything, down to imported beer and designer clothes. The money, however usually comes from you. In the beginning, they will not dream of letting you spend a cent. Very soon, however, there are little excuses for borrowing cash. A cash flow problem soon becomes ongoing.

Absence of close friends. The con is usually a loner. While he may be very personable and appear to know everyone around him, he has few, if any, intimate friends. He will develop "friendships" with casual acquaintances, store clerks, waitpersons, etc.,. in the event that he may require their assistance in the future. He often has a following of people on whom he can call for favors. However, the length of these associations are brief. He will eventually call upon them for monetary favors, such as cashing a check that he can not cover. He does not allow anyone to get too close or to know too much about his actual life.

Inconsistent work history. No self-respecting con man will remain in a work intensive job for any length of time. Many avoid work entirely, living off the exploits of their victims. Others are attracted to jobs such as sales that allow them freedom of movement. Their employment history, however, will be sporadic with much movement from job to job, and periods of unemployment. Gambling is perceived as an effortless form of income.

If any or all of the above red flags is present in your relationship, run, don't walk, to the nearest exit.

Learned Behavior

In Part II we discussed the case of Chuck, who associated gambling with his father. Association, the tendency to connect things that occur together in space and time, is the key to learning theory. Ivan Pavlov (1927) referred to this as classical conditioning.

Classical conditioning occurs in humans when they connect a stimulus, such as food, with another stimulus, such as a bell or tuning fork. Food elicits an automatic physiological response. When we see and smell food, we feel hungry. If the fire whistle blew at the same time everyday just before lunch was served, we would then begin to feel hungry as a response to the fire whistle because we would have learned to associate the whistle with the food.

Chuck felt excitement and love being with his father. The times that they spent together were at the racetrack. Chuck developed a conditioned association for the racetrack. The track elicited in Chuck the positive feelings he felt when he was on an outing with his dad.

Another form of conditioning, according to Skinner (1938), is operant conditioning. Operant conditioning is the association of a reward or punishment with an action. Skinner believed that we repeat actions that are rewarded, and decrease actions that are punished.

We can also learn behavior through negative reinforcement, which is the removal of an unpleasant stimulus by the use of a certain action. We learn that by taking an aspirin or other pain reducer, we can alleviate a headache.

Jackie was feeling depressed and anxious. She hated her job and her roommate. At the end of a miserable day, she hated going home because her roommate would be there. She discovered that by playing the slot machines she could temporarily ease her tensions.

"When I sit down at the machine, all my worries go away. I feel great."

Jackie had become conditioned to use gambling as a form of medication for her emotional stress.

The casinos have built-in stimuli designed to increase the conditioning response. For example, the lights, bells, and colorful fruit activate the part of your nervous system that provides stimulation. We quickly associate that excitement with pleasure. We learn that we can feel good when we are in that environment. We naturally want to return to a place that causes us to feel good.

When we win, we also have an automatic excitation reaction. Even if we see someone near us win, we are reinforced by their excitement.

You might think that losing would act as a negative, reducing your positive association. However, the casinos use random reinforcement in a way that reduces extinction. Extinction, the discontinuation of a conditioned response, occurs when the reinforcer is no longer present. We expect our painkiller to eliminate our headache or reduce our fever whenever we use it. If I can no longer get relief from aspirin, I might begin to try other forms of pain reducers.

Random reinforcement, however, makes it harder to eliminate the conditioned response. For example, if I won every time I put a quarter in a slot machine, I would more likely quit the first time or two that I did not win. However, slots are set to pay off on a random schedule. We know it will pay off sometime, we just don't know when. It might not pay off for hours or even days. Then, it might pay off several times in a row.

Consequently, if we do not win, we continue to play in the knowledge that eventually it will pay off. This is why slot machine players have such difficulty overcoming their habit, even after they realize they are losing money.

Finally, another form of learned behavior occurs through modeling, or observational learning (Bandura, 1986). Modeling is the repetition of behavior that we observe in those who act as our reference group. In most cases this is our family. If we grow up watching our parents or siblings use gambling as a form of entertainment or as a method of coping with stress, we learn this form of behavior. Sometimes the observed behavior can be generalized.

Pete's mother is a compulsive spender. She loves spending money and buying presents. When she is shopping, she is in a form of action. Pete also likes to spend money, and he finds that gambling provides a similar form of excitement. He is an action gambler, who gambles on sports, blackjack, craps, and horses. Like his mother, he loves to be in action.

Learning theory is the nurture aspect of the nature/nurture argument. They should not be viewed, however, as an either/or. While some individuals may have physiological predispositions toward gambling, and while gambling activates certain neurotransmitters in the brain, we cannot ignore the learning component. Rather than perceiving gambling as nature or nurture, it is more likely that the two work in a synergy with one another, much like love and sexual attraction.

Part IV

WHAT? Implications and factors

The first three sections have provided an overview of gambling, its causes and demographic differences. This section will discuss some of the implications and factors of problem gambling, including the impact of gambling on ones personal, spiritual and social lives. In addition, legal and financial issues will be examined.

Spiritual: Connectedness

He who has a why to live for can bear almost any how.
Nietzsche

Who am I? What do I want from life? What do I value? Whom do I care about? These are the questions that must be asked and answered before we can feel connected.

Victor Frankl (1959) states that the essence of human existence is responsibleness, and that we discover meaning in life in three ways: by creating a work or doing a deed; by expressing something or encountering someone; or by the attitude we take toward unavoidable suffering

The gambler operates on a purely hedonistic level. He acts and reacts according to the throw of the dice or the draw of the card at that particular moment in time. He lives in a dream world driven by the fantasy of the big win. His energy and focus are directed toward one end, the action.

For the gambler, relationships serve to support the overall goal, to continue gambling. Individuals may share the excitement and gambling activity, they may provide money and resources, or they may be part of the overall perpetuation of the illusion. There may be little or no guilt over the harm perpetrated on another because it is only temporary. In the end everything will be wonderful. All will be forgiven.

Victor Frankl (1959) tells us that without meaning in our lives, we suffer a void. Such a void can lead to depression, aggression, or addiction. We know that we often self medicate our anxieties with alcohol, drugs, or gambling. According to Frankl, we may be attempting to replace meaning with meaningless activity.

Our society has slowly replaced creativity with passive entertainment. Our parents or grandparents may be able to remember the pleasure of reading a book, gazing into a fire as their imaginations flowed freely, or building a tree fort out of foraged wood and discarded boxes. Today, we expect to be entertained through machines and visual imagery. We no longer are in touch with our own inner abilities. We eschew books for videos or compact discs that require nothing from us and make no connection to our internal resources. Entertainment is prepackaged and predetermined. We are passive participants in our own entertainment.

The gambler is but one of the results of such disconnection. The gambler expects instant excitement, instant gratification. It must be loud, colorful, and intense. It must require little more than money. Any skill involved is more a delusion than a reality. It is, however, all consuming. And while engaging in it, the gambler does not feel the void.

When the gambler enters recovery there is a sense of disconnectedness, a lack of purpose in life. He is, once again, faced with the overwhelming void of meaning. In order to become connected, the gambler must get in touch with himself, with the external world, and with those around him. For some it may involve reconnecting to a self that had been lost, others may need to develop a connection that never existed.

Joe had been gambling on a daily basis since his late teens. He was now 37. His social environment consisted of gambling related activities. He reached low bottom three weeks after his girlfriend threw him out of their apartment. When she left his bags on the front lawn, he shrugged off his disappointment and moved in with his parents. After a week he found the stress of hiding his gambling activity too difficult and moved to a motel. Joe had always managed to work during the day. He made good money in construction, which enabled him to gamble regularly. A long losing streak left him without gambling funds, however, and he began taking money from the construction trailer where the company kept enough to cash workers' checks. He was convinced that the next win would enable him to put the money back before it was needed at the end of the pay period. Joe's losing streak continued, and the missing money was discovered before he could return it. A process of elimination identified Joe as the culprit.

The foreman had been Joe's friend for ten years and was hesitant to turn him in, but the money had to be returned. Joe had no alternative, but to go to his parents. Joe's parents talked with his girlfriend who enlightened them about Joe's gambling problem. They agreed to pay back the money provided that Joe went to Gamblers Anonymous (GA) and stopped gambling. At the advice of a gambling counselor, his parents took over control of Joe's finances, taking out the money he owed them and giving him just enough cash to live on. Joe avoided incarceration, but he lost his job and went on unemployment. He moved back in with his parents.

Joe went into recovery with a frenzy, attending GA meetings three times a week. He was driven to convince his family that he had recovered. Joe was certain that he would never gamble again. Everything was OK. He was cured.

One evening he sat in a bar, nursing a beer, and watching a shuffleboard game. A man sat down beside him and they began to talk. During the course of conversation, the man asked him about his hobbies. Joe was flabbergasted. Hobbies? He had no hobbies. For his entire adult life, his focus had been on gambling. He realized he would need to completely rebuild his identity. Joe knew then that his recovery was going to be harder than he had imagined.

The first step in Joe's rebirth required him to develop a sense of self-respect. When he looked into the mirror, he saw himself as his parents and former girlfriend must view him. He had let them down. He was a failure. He wanted them to see him in a new light, as responsible and honorable. Frankl describes responsibleness as the essence of human existence. Joe needed to find that essence.

Joe began to work temporary construction jobs to enable him to pay back his parents. He continued to turn over his pay to his mother, who gave him a weekly allowance. There were many evenings that Joe paced the perimeter of his parents' home, feeling as though he would erupt from the tedium of his life. Often he felt there was no hope.

He forced himself to visualize the image he wanted to present to his parents. Each day became slightly easier.

Joe desperately wanted to feel connected romantically. He tried to recapture the relationship with his girlfriend. One evening he called and asked to see her. She agreed. Joe told her of his hope to construct a new, more responsible self. She listened politely, but told him that her feelings for him were not strong enough to sustain the challenges presented to the relationship. She wished him well, but it was over.

Joe expected to be devastated by her dictum, but as he drove away he felt relief. Joe realized that he needed to start anew. The person she had known was not the person he wanted to be. He needed to begin a relationship that was founded on a more equal plane, and one that emerged from mutual interests and values. He still wasn't sure what those values were, however.

Joe's next step was to discover some interest in life, some pleasurable pursuit outside of gambling. He remembered that, as a small child, he loved to fish. Joe borrowed his father's fishing gear and went to a nearby river. There he got in touch with the physical plane in a quiet, unrushed manner.

As Joe sat on the riverbank alone he allowed himself to experience the physical sensations that he had not taken the time to notice for many years. He felt the coolness of the grass, and heard the many sounds of nature. He lay back on the bank and watched the sky as it changed in hue. He smelled the earth and water. Once, he caught a small fish and felt its slippery, scaled body before throwing it back into the river with a tiny plop. This was what Joe might have perceived as inactivity in the past. The hours spent on that riverbank, though, were more sensually active and alive than anything he had experienced since childhood.

Joe's father was a carpenter and spent much time building cabinets and furniture of wood. Joe began to spend time watching his father, occasionally pitching in to help. Soon he found that he enjoyed finishing the wood, sanding, staining, and polishing. The activity gave him a great deal of satisfaction.

Joe's relationship with his father developed a new depth. He began to see his father in a new light, as a creative, capable individual, as an artist. Joe and his father shared stories and laughed together during their hours in the workshop. A meaningful relationship was being forged.

Joe was pleased with the newly found connection to his father, but he still longed for a romantic relationship. Joe began to realize, however, that in order to connect to another person, he had to be able to connect to himself. He needed to know who he was and what he wanted before he would know what to look for in another individual and what he was capable of giving.

Before Joe began his journey of self-discovery, his connection with strangers involved sports scores, predictions, and gambling stories. At a recent family picnic, that involved extended relatives and friends, Joe found himself talking to a woman about the variation of the colors of the sky at dawn and at sunset. Joe shared his thoughts and emotions spontaneously without any preconceived intent to impress or concern about her reaction. The total experience was extremely intimate and satisfying for both of them.

The gambler shares on a superficial level. His goal is usually to raise his status in the eyes of the listener. The words may involve truth or lies, but they have little meaning.

In order to connect with another individual, we must move from asking what they can do for us, or how can we hide our secrets, to what can we share that has true meaning.

Here are five valuable questions to ask and be prepared to answer:
- What are your thoughts, beliefs, and philosophies?
- What are your feelings, fears, and wishes?
- What are your values, involvements?

- What are your passions?
- How can I enhance your world?

Needless to say, the questions may be couched in appropriate context and terminology. However, the intention is to learn and to share, not to impress or fill time. If you discover that your interests and beliefs are too polarized, you may not wish to continue the relationship. Nevertheless, you have had an interesting conversation and have probably learned something new.

For Joe, the journey toward connectedness had only begun. There would be many days when the struggle would seem too overwhelming, and he would crave the action and escape from reality that gambling had provided.

Gamblers fill the void in their lives with superficial promises, lacking substance and purpose. For recovery to occur, the gambler must move from a world of existence, and begin the process of connecting to himself and to those around him. He must create a new life of meaning and depth. This process is not quick or facile. It can not be accomplished in a few exciting minutes, but takes a lifetime of exploration in infinitesimal, painstaking, steps, beginning with one deep breath.

Personal Factors: Shame and Anger

"I'm so ashamed." This is a recurring statement among gamblers. Deep, shameful feelings drive individuals to contemplate suicide, to lie, and to commit illegal acts in an attempt to prevent discovery.

The spouse, parent, or loved one often continues to enable the gambler, bailing him out and protecting him because of the overwhelming shame. True, the actions are motivated in part by love. You don't want to see your loved one suffering. Often, however, the behaviors are motivated by the desire to hide, to avoid the shame.

Lois discovered that her husband, Roy, had run up thousands on their credit cards. She feared they would lose their home. She felt rage toward Roy.

She kept repeating, "What if someone were to find out? I couldn't face anyone, ever again. How can I tell my mother?" Lois was fearful for their financial situation, but mostly she feared coping with the shame of others knowing she had married a pathological gambler.

Roy admitted he had lied to cover up the extent of his gambling. He'd thought about going to gamblers' anonymous, but was afraid that Lois would find out.

"I couldn't face her," he said. "I was so ashamed."

In fact, Lois had discovered the credit cards by accident. Roy had been getting the mail, but she came home early one day and discovered the bills. Roy admitted that part of his escalation in gambling was due to his attempt to win enough to pay off the cards so that she would never need to know what he had done.

When Lois and Roy entered counseling, it was difficult for them to discuss their situation. The shame that Lois felt intensified Roy's personal shame and made it hard for him to talk to her about it. Lois was angry with Roy because she felt she had been publicly humiliated.

Shame is not necessarily a bad thing. Constructively, shame acts as a feedback mechanism to inhibit us from engaging in acts that could harm others and, thereby, damage our self-image. Constructive shame provides us with a sense of sadness that motivates us to atone for past wrongs. When we feel bad about past behaviors, and learn from them, it encourages spiritual growth.

However, shame can be destructive. Destructive shame is irrational and disempowering. It damages our self-image unnecessarily without allowing for the growth process of atonement. Destructive shame is based on unrealistic expectations that have been imposed upon us by others.

Triggers to destructive shame are self-imposed judgments from our past: We must not make mistakes. We cannot be less than perfect, or someone will not love us.

Lois feared being judged by her family and friends. Although she, herself, had not gambled, Roy was her husband.

We often experience shame through the actions of those close to us. We feel shame if a loved one has run up debt, or if we are forced into bankruptcy due to the actions of a family member. If our children do not succeed, or our spouses are abusive, it becomes our shame.

Destructive shame is secretive. We hide the bruises of abuse, whether physical, financial, or emotional. Our fear of discovery fuels the intensity of our shameful feelings, obstructing the healing process.

It is important for us to identify those feelings of shame, and to be able to categorize them as constructive or destructive. If we are responsible for behaviors that have incurred shameful feelings, then we can ask the questions: Am I sorry for those actions? Have I done what I could to stop the behaviors? Am I atoning for those actions in any way? If we have done what we could to rectify our behaviors, then we need to allow ourselves the right to relinquish the feelings of shame.

If the shame is the result of the actions of others, then we need to allow those individuals to take responsibility for their own behaviors. By taking the responsibility for them, we are preventing them from experiencing their own growth and healing.

When Lois first discovered Roy's gambling losses, she took charge. She called the credit card companies; she consulted a consumer credit bureau. The more Lois did to rectify the problem that Roy had created, the more he retreated into his dark and shameful cavern.

Lois admitted that she resented cleaning up the mess that Roy had created. She reluctantly acknowledged that the main source of her motivation was that she wanted to ensure that no one would find out. She agreed to permit Roy to take some of the responsibility for cleaning up his own mess.

Lois and Roy also agreed to confront their fear of discovery. At the urge of the counselor, they selected key family members and friends to talk to about Roy's gambling. Surprisingly, most of the people they confided in were extremely supportive. When the public ostracism did not occur as expected, both of them began to experience a sense of relief and freedom.

"It felt so good to be able to talk to someone without fear," Lois reported.

Roy smiled when he said, "I used to feel like gum on the bottom of my shoe. Now, I think maybe I'm not quite that bad. A lot of people make mistakes. When I tell them I have a gambling problem, they tell me about their problem. I still feel bad, but not so bad." He grinned at Lois who was holding his hand.

We need to understand that shame and guilt, while closely related, and often used interchangeably, are not necessarily the same. Webster's Dictionary defines guilt as "a feeling of self reproach from believing that one has done a wrong." Shame is defined as "dishonor or disgrace".

While we often experience both guilt and shame, we can experience shame without guilt. We may not feel at all guilty about our actions while gambling, but experience intense shame when we are discovered. Narcissists feel little guilt or remorse, but experience agonizing shame.

They want to be seen by the public in a positive light, and are easily intimidated by negative public responses. They feel little to no remorse, however, as long as they remain undiscovered.

We can undo feelings of guilt through actions of atonement. We may always feel shame, however, unless we openly address the underlying causes of those shameful feelings. Confronting our fears can be extremely difficult, but is rejuvenating and heartening.

Someone said that bravery is not an absence of fear, but action in the face of fear. It takes much more courage to overcome our mistakes than to live a life free from error.

The surprising benefit is that by freely and openly acknowledging the behavior and by taking pride in our efforts to rehabilitate our actions, we intensify the healing process. The first step is the hardest, but the most important. The following list of exercises will assist you in ridding yourself of destructive shame.

- Make a list of unrealistic beliefs from your past that encourages shameful feelings. For example, I must get all As in school or my parents would be disappointed, or if I went out of the house without my makeup on and someone saw me, they would think I was terrible. You may need to start a journal, or diary to assist you in processing these memories. Or, you may ask a childhood friend or relative to work with you.

- Identify areas where you are taking responsibility for another's actions. Are your feelings of shame related to the behavior of those close to you, rather than to something you, yourself, have done? Avoid apologizing when your children, parents, spouse, friends, do something you see as inappropriate. Allow them to take responsibility for their own actions. Ask yourself, why should I be ashamed because of what they did?

- Identify ways in which you can openly confront your own shame. Make a list of the people you could tell beginning with the hardest and working down to the easiest. Start at the bottom of the list and work upward at your own pace. When you find yourself stuck, visualize the conversation. Image how you will feel when you have confronted your fear. Imagine walking away from the conversation feeling healthier and more at peace with yourself.

•   Develop your own treatment plan for coping with shame. List the things you believe will assist you in overcoming your destructive shame,

Anger, like pain, is a built-in safety mechanism that lets you know something is not right. It acts as a feedback mechanism to get you back on track. Unfortunately, however, we don't always recognize our feelings of anger. Sometimes we misidentify those feelings and, therefore, displace them. Often we turn our anger inward and become depressed, or we strike out at ourselves in self-destructive ways.

Obviously, it is not beneficial to misdirect anger. Consequently, we need to learn how to accurately identify our feelings of anger and the source of those feelings.

Some of us are taught that it is not good to experience anger. Many women have been taught that it is "unladylike" or unappealing. People won't like us if we express anger. So we learn to suppress our feelings of anger.

In addition, feelings of anger toward a loved one create a sense of cognitive dissonance. I love him. I am angry with him. How can I love him if I am angry with him? Perhaps then I don't love him. If I am angry with him, then I should do something. What can I do? I am afraid to do something? I might lose him. The end result is that it is easier to ignore the anger.

Difficulty expressing anger can interfere with assertive setting of boundaries in a relationship. Likewise, difficulty in identifying anger can interfere with self-preservation.

Gregg confronted his gambling problem after losing over $100,000. He and his wife were forced into bankruptcy and had to take out a mortgage on their home of 30 years. The home had been paid off prior to the gambling debt, and the couple was planning their retirement. Gregg's wife, Nancy, threatened divorce, but ultimately remained in the marriage. She was furious with Gregg, however, and expressed her wrath at every opportunity.

At first, Gregg was overwhelmed with guilt. He welcomed Nancy's tirades as due penance for his sins. Weeks passed and Gregg began feeling more and more depressed. He began to believe that he would never be able to atone for his transgressions. He started spending more and more time alone. He would go for long walks and sit on park benches, staring into space.

Gregg had never been a drinker. He would have an occasional drink with dinner, but seldom went to bars. One day, on one of his walks, he wandered into a bar. He started with beer, and progressed to whiskey. Fortunately, he wasn't driving. He was sick for three days.

Gregg didn't continue drinking, but he stopped taking care of himself. He ate very little, started smoking (he had quit ten years earlier), and stayed awake most of the night watching old movies.

After several months of self-destructive behavior, Nancy insisted that Gregg go to counseling. It was during the counseling session that Gregg's anger began to surface.

"Why doesn't anyone understand?" he kept asking. "Do they all think that I wanted to ruin our lives? Don't all the years that I went to work, brought home my pay check, never cheated, don't they count?"

Once he got started, Gregg raged at the casinos that continued to advance his credit, his parents who had stopped speaking to him, his wife, and his son.

"I know that what I did was wrong. I know that I made a mistake. Nancy deserves to be angry, but doesn't anyone understand that I couldn't help what I did?"

Gregg was shocked that he could get so deeply in debt in such a short time. He couldn't believe that he had so little control over his behavior. His feelings of frustration over his inability to repair the damage that he had done and his rage at the situation were overwhelming to him.

Gregg had been displacing his feelings of anger by turning them into depression and self-abuse. He felt that if he could hurt himself enough that he would be purged of his guilt and pain.

Nancy's anger was also multifaceted. Yes, she was angry with Gregg, and he received the brunt of her wrath. However, she was also angry at the casinos and credit card companies. Most of all, she was angry at the injustice. This was a time in their lives when they should be thinking of retirement. How could this be happening now? She was immobilized by frustration fueled by her inability to fix this situation.

Nancy had always been a fixer. She could straighten out problems, conflicts, anything, if given enough time. There was no fixing this problem.

Most of her fury at Gregg centered on her belief that Gregg had consciously chosen to gamble away their life savings. If he had been overcome by a physical illness, or he had lost his job due to economic factors, she could have coped. She was convinced, however, that this devastation was self-inflicted. Nancy was not able to comprehend the power of the gambling addiction, or to view it as a disease. For her, Gregg's was a voluntary act, and as such, unforgivable.

Anger is usually related to our perception or belief about a situation. If someone bumps into me because he tripped, I am not angry. If, on the other hand, I do not see him trip, and I believe that he purposefully bumped me, then I become angry. A change in perception, or belief about an event can easily alter our emotional response.

In general, nonassertive behavior can lead to anger. We allow our boundaries or basic rights to be violated without taking a firm position to protect them. Such lack of action on our part, then, damages our self-esteem. We either become depressed, or we begin to feel angry. Therefore, the next event that is perceived as a violation of our rights is the basis for an aggressive, hostile outburst. By maintaining our boundaries assertively from the start, we can avoid such destructive feelings.

Anger can have a devastating impact on a relationship. Communication becomes defensive or hostile. Sexual desire is inhibited.

All conflicts that should be managed through problem solving become a forum for venting your wrath. Eventually, the anger is reciprocated and a wall of resentment has been constructed.

So far, anger looks pretty destructive. Perhaps we should avoid it altogether? On the contrary, as we said in the beginning of the chapter, anger can serve as a feedback mechanism that provides us with fair warning that something needs attention. Like the red stoplight, anger is not to be ignored. Here are some guidelines to follow in utilizing anger to your advantage:

• Take its temperature. If your anger is totally out of control, at the rage level, you are probably reacting to something that has a strong emotional connotation for you. When this happens you first need to get control. Take a few deep breaths and remove yourself from the situation until you calm down. Then begin to inventory the possible connections between the overt trigger of your anger and the underlying cause. Some of the common causes of intense anger include a sense of injustice, betrayal, fear of abandonment, fear of helplessness, or financial ruin. Underlying these sources are some irrational thoughts or personal insecurities that must be addressed; i.e., I will never be loved again, the world is unfair, I will never recover, etc.

• Find the boundary. Anger usually indicates a boundary violation. What, is the personal boundary that has been violated? It is critical that you do not allow your boundaries to be transgressed repeatedly without consequence. Once they have been identified, establish the consequences for future violations. Be firm. In training children, we can easily identify those behaviors, which we will not tolerate. We develop clear-cut rules of behavior. We then teach our children the consequences for breaking our rules. We must do the same with the adults in our lives. We identify our basic boundaries, let those close to us know what they are, and establish consequences when they are breached.

• Take control. There is nothing worse than feeling out of control of your life. Often we feel we have no alternatives, but there are always choices. Sometimes we don't want to exercise those choices, but to not do so is to continue with the sense of helplessness, rage, or depression. Taking control does not always have to be a major leap. Sometimes incremental changes in our patterns can produce a sense of empowerment.

Grace feared that her husband, George, would abandon her, leaving her penniless. Each time he gambled away the rent money, her fear intensified. George usually managed to pay the rent eventually, but it was this fear that fed Grace's anger. Grace began taking small sums of money from her household accounts. She started a savings account in her name only. Each week she would put a few dollars in the account. It wasn't much, but it gave her some sense of control. The empowerment she began to experience eventually enabled her to confront George about his gambling and to insist that she be given total control over the household finances. George was so shocked at Grace's assertiveness that he agreed to give her a household account, and to put enough money in the account to pay their household bills each month. When he did gamble all of his money, at least she felt secure that they would not be evicted.

Listen to your anger. It's telling you something. If you run a marathon with knee pain, you will suffer an injury. If you ignore your anger it will only intensify, or turn against you.

Overall, anger can be devastating to your physical and mental well-being. On the other hand, anger can act as a form of constructive feedback that allows you to identify areas that require adjustment. By taking control over your life, you can learn to direct your anger so that it works for you, rather than against you.

Relational Implications

You may wonder why anyone would want to remain in a relationship with someone who had destroyed their financial security and betrayed their trust. Yet, people choose to stay in a relationship for many reasons. It is important to note here that not all individuals who remain in such relationships are "co-dependent" or lifetime victims. As a society, we have a tendency to blame the victim.

We are quick to attach a label of co-dependence on a woman who remains with a gambling spouse, but we are less quick to so label the husband who remains with his gambling wife. It does seem to follow, however, that women are more likely to remain with a gambling spouse than men.

Most of the husbands of gamblers I have encountered want the problem "fixed" quickly. They are also less interested in attending counseling. They are more likely to perceive the problem as her's alone. Ironically, the majority of married female gamblers I have seen complain of emotionally absent spouses.

For those who attempt to salvage their marriages, the relationship often represents the majority of their adult lives. They may find it impossible to imagine life without the other. For some, the financial burden, which is stressed with the spouse, is perceived as even worse without him. And, of course, there is that overused, but inevitable word "love."

Many state that, with the exception of gambling, their partner has always been loving, caring, and a joy to be with. They want that pre-gambling person back.

We need to differentiate between those who are attracted to and marry gamblers, and those for whom gambling entered their lives after marriage.

Action gamblers can be very charming and exciting to be around. It doesn't take long, though, before that excitement begins to become wearing.

For individuals who grew up in dysfunctional families, however, the abnormal is perceived as the norm. Some as ordinary may perceive those characteristics, which many of us would identify as aberrant. Their systems have become adjusted to constant arousal, even if it is negative. These individuals may, on some level, wish to continue the roller coaster lifestyle, which the gambler has provided, and find it almost as difficult to recover as the gambler.

Mark and Sheila were married in Vegas. Their lives were a constant whirlwind of casinos, card games, nightclubs, and glitter. Sheila never gambled, but she loved to stay in the casinos where Mark was comped (compensated) with free rooms, food, and drink. She bought expensive clothes in the hotel boutiques, and spent hours in lavish restaurants, seeing shows, and watching Mark gamble. She had no idea how much money he spent, or where the money came from to pay their debts. She knew only that they always seemed to have more than they needed.

Mark was a salesman who spent most of his time setting up card games, sports bets, and casino trips. Mark gambled on anything and everything. For the first five years of their marriage, Mark stayed ahead, winning consistently. Then his luck changed. By the time he entered his first GA meeting, Mark was in debt for over $200,000. Their house was mortgaged twice, and they owned nothing. Sheila was shocked when she discovered their financial situation, but was even more shocked when she was told that they would be forced to end their life style. It was over. No more fancy restaurants, boutiques, or hotel rooms.

Sheila had not worked since her marriage. She had been forced to quit school right after high school to care for her father, who was an alcoholic. Sheila's mother had left home when she was a baby. Sheila was accustomed to her father's mood swings and eccentricities. When she met Mark, she saw nothing unusual in his somewhat irresponsible lifestyle. Mark insisted that she spend her time taking care of him rather than working at a paying job. She was happy to comply with his wishes.

When Mark quit gambling, Sheila obtained work as a clerk in a clothing store. Mark lost his sales job and went to work for his family's florist business. They lost their home and moved in with Mark's parents. Sheila grieved her lost lifestyle. Mark was not the exciting man she had married.

Susan and Mike had a good marriage before Mike's gambling. They had met in college and Susan was attracted to Mike's maturity and sense of responsibility. They shared everything together, supported each other's dreams, and consoled each other in their disappointments. Even in the midst of her anger at his deception regarding his gambling activities, Susan could not fathom a life without Mike. Her major fears were not for financial disaster, but for the loss of intimacy. She wanted to trust and believe in Mike again. She wanted to feel affection for him, but she was afraid. His betrayal had thrust a wedge between them that she feared could never be removed.

Both Susan and Sheila stayed with their gamblers. For Susan, the relationship was valuable enough to work out their problems. For Sheila, she perceived their reduced lifestyle to be, nevertheless, an improvement over life alone.

The first step for both couples was for them to be able to talk to each other. Mark and Sheila had communicated through activities and material objects. They laughed, they joked, and they had sex. They talked about the wins (sometimes the losses), the shows they saw, the food they ate, the people they encountered. At no time did they ever communicate their fears, or inner desires, or share emotions. For Mark and Sheila, communication was tantamount to learning a new language.

Susan and Mike shared many thoughts and very deep feelings, except one, anger. Susan had never been able to express her anger toward Mike, other than on a very superficial level. She could blow up over something trivial, such as Mike's spending too much on her birthday present. She did not, however, find that she could share with him deep feelings of hurt and disappointment. Susan an expression of such feelings would be a declaration of disloyalty. Love equaled support. They could easily disagree on an intellectual level about philosophical issues, but not about personal ones.

Both Susan and Sheila needed to be able to identify their expectations in order to establish clear boundaries. These boundaries would define for them when their gambler had crossed the line. Once defined they then needed to be able to communicate what the boundaries were, what behaviors were unacceptable, and what would be the consequences for violating those boundaries

As individuals, we each have our own issues and concerns. There are two areas that are consistent among all couples coping with gambling addiction: money, and honesty.

The next section will address in detail the issues related to money. The importance of money in the reconnecting couple is predominately one of empowerment. Ironically, the non-gambling spouse must be capable of leaving in order to be able to stay. This requires her to set up a system of safeguards that will ensure her financial safety and independence.

The gambler has been accustomed to playing the hero with money, bringing home presents, and providing a comfortable lifestyle. Now, in order for the spouse to feel secure, he must turn over all control of the finances. She will need to establish solid assertive communication techniques in order to be able to maintain this financial system. The pitfall here is that such an arrangement places the spouse in a parental role. Parenting one's spouse is not likely to lead to intimacy. Nevertheless this is a necessary evil if she is to be able to sleep at night without worry over what he might do next, or whether they will be evicted at any moment.

The temptation for many women is to use this control as a club, a way to express years of pent up anger and resentment. Such a power play is not likely to lead to intimacy.

The gambling spouse will use all his tricks to persuade his wife to relinquish her control over finances. He will manipulate her, using her love for him, or her desire to please him.

It is necessary that the spouse dance the line between assertive monitoring of money and a vengeful power play. Here are some assertive responses to likely statements and questions from the gambling spouse when he wants to break the rules regarding control over money:

Question: "Don't you trust me?"

Response: "Why take the chance? I think it would be safer this way. Let's stick to the plan."

Statement: "I need to prove to myself that I can handle money again."

Response: "We have an agreement. Let's stick to it."

Statement: "Why are you being so stubborn about this."?

Response: "I'm sorry you feel that way, but I would feel safer if we just stick with the plan."

It is always a safe bet to merely repeat, "Let's just stick to the plan.

"If you are feeling truly compassionate, you can always respond with "I know how hard it is for you. You are doing so well. You can do it. I know you can."

Resist the pressure to engage in a debate. The gambler usually wins those. If really pushed to the wall say, "Let's see what the other GA members think." That will usually put a stop to it. He knows exactly what the GA members will say.

Most importantly, avoid sarcasm. Do not say, "Trust you? Are you kidding?"

Assertive communication is difficult to maintain in the beginning. Old habits are hard to break. Conflict management strategies such as avoidance, accommodating, or competition are much easier to continue. However, once learned, assertive techniques increase self-esteem and are much more empowering and comfortable, and less likely to lead to hostility or hurt.

The second boundary, which must be enforced, is honesty. The gambler has learned to become comfortable with lies. It has become a way of life. This rule is harder to enforce that money because it is not as easy to monitor. Nevertheless, the gambler must begin to recognize the value of honesty and its importance in the relationship.

Heretofore, the attitude has been, "What she doesn't know won't hurt her." We all know that these are the hurts that cause the deepest wounds. They are felt as betrayal.

Why does he have to lie? This is a common question from those for whom lies are usually limited to not hurting someone's feelings, or lies of omission. For many of us, telling lies creates anxiety and dissonance. We are uncomfortable, and usually show some visual reaction such as blushing or even hives. Some of us cannot tell a lie without averting our eyes or changing our vocal tone. Many of us exercise adaptors, nonverbal indicators that we are tense, such as tapping our feet or twirling our hair. We find it difficult to understand why someone cannot only lie easily, but prefers to lie when it does not seem necessary.

For the gambler, lying quickly becomes a way of life, if it wasn't before. Secrecy and isolation become the policy in an overall effort to hide the gambling activity. There are some gamblers who only lie about gambling, and others who lie about everything. For most, however, the lies become so confused with reality, they lose the ability to differentiate.

Jack's mother adored him. She described him to her friends as perfect in all ways. He was never disciplined, because he did no wrong. Jack quickly learned that his mother did not want to know of his imperfections. He could not bear to see any indication that she was disappointed in him. Therefore, Jack learned at an early age to hide his mistakes. If he forgot to do something she had asked, he covered it up, telling her that he had completed the task. Or, if he couldn't cover it up, he blamed his negligence on someone else. For Jack, being perfect became his goal in life. He would lie, and embellish the lies, in order to ensure that he maintained his perfect image.

Jack perceived gambling as acceptable as long as he won. Therefore, he would lie about his losses and exaggerate his wins. If he met with any resistance to the many hours he spent gambling, he would lie about that, too.

Jack was not satisfied with merely lying to cover up the truth; he needed to embellish the lies to convince not only the listener, but also himself. For Jack, the lies became the reality. If he told the lie often enough and well enough, he would then be able to believe it himself.

Kurt, on the other hand, knew exactly what he was doing when he lied. He wanted to gamble. Kurt was an action gambler who couldn't breathe unless he was gambling. Kurt's wife, Sarah, and Kurt's boss began to complain about the time Kurt spent gambling. Kurt became obsessed with his cover-up stories. He hid his gambling money in several places where his wife wouldn't find it, such as the toe of his gym shoes, or a musty old book on fly-fishing. He would conjure up evening projects, such as community action committees, in order to cover up his time away from home. Kurt even pretended to go to a GA meeting weekly. He had gambling buddies call his home to tell him a work project needed his attention.

Kurt's wife attempted to go with Kurt to the racetrack in an effort to moderate his gambling. Kurt promised to limit the money gambled to a certain amount. Kurt would go to the men's room, and then sneak to another floor to place large bets while pretending to stay within his budget. There was no limit to Kurt's ingenuity when it came to protecting his secret. Kurt's covert gambling life became his primary objective.

For Kurt, and many others, the lies were rationalized and supported by other gamblers who insisted that their spouses just didn't understand. It became a joke, a game. After a while, it became an obsession.

Mike began lying to Susan when he realized that his gambling had become a problem. He was less concerned with perpetuating the activity than he was in perpetuating her image of him as a good guy, a smart guy, and a responsible guy. For a long time, Mike believed that he could recoup his losses, thereby justifying the lies. He promised himself he would tell all as soon as he could demonstrate that he made it all right.

Mike was not as comfortable with the lies as Kurt or Jack, and consequently, he subconsciously sabotaged himself. He allowed a credit card bill to come to the house so that Susan would find it. Mike claimed that he thought he could retrieve the bill before Susan saw it, but he was actually relieved when the truth came out.

Mike had stopped gambling for several months. One week, when Susan and the kids were visiting relatives, Mike relapsed. He hid the relapse from Susan, thinking that if she didn't know then she wouldn't be disappointed in him. When she discovered the relapse, he found it difficult to understand that her disappointment was due more to the lie than to the relapse.

Mike actually relapsed again several months later, but immediately told Susan and then went to a GA meeting. Susan was sorry that Mike relapsed, but pleased that he told her the truth. They discussed preventive measures without hostility. Mike began to gain some insight into the value of honesty at that point in time. He described it as a relief to be able to share his urges and fears with Susan without worry that she would reject him or chastise him. For Mike, honesty became a refuge and a comfort.

For the action gambler, the lying and secrecy become part of the overall excitement of gambling. Living on the edge, with the constant fear of discovery, adds an element of danger that heightens the action. The action gambler is addicted to the excitement. He will need to sacrifice the lies as part of the total package in order to withdraw from his addiction. Some will substitute other deceptions, such as affairs, to maintain the excitement.

Other gamblers experience a profound sense of relief when they no longer need to lie to cover up their gambling activities. Gloria would look her children in the eye and lie about where she had been. The guilt she felt was so intense that she would avoid them, waiting until they were asleep before coming home after gambling. When she finally got control over her addiction, she said that the joy she felt when she could, once again, look at her children and speak to them honestly was so satisfying that it was keeping her from relapsing.

The gambler must begin to examine the source of his lies and the purpose of maintaining them. What do they do for him? What form of self-protection do they provide? When did he begin lying on a frequent basis?

Many gamblers will initially provide pat responses, such as not wanting to hurt the spouse, or feeling embarrassed. While these reasons may be true, they are probably not the total cause of the lies. The gambler may have never acknowledged the actual benefits of lying. Identifying the source of the lies may be the most complex problem to treat because it can involve long-term analysis of past patterns and development. Most gambling treatment is short-term and will not engage that deeply. Therefore, cognitive-behavioral approaches are more frequently used, which focus on the more immediate benefits of honesty.

In some cases, however, the couple joins forces to perpetuate their lies to themselves as well as to each other. Helen and Leonard were both gamblers, they began gambling together, and together they escalated their addiction. Each was convinced that they were keeping the other company.

On weekends Helen would ask Leonard what he wanted to do, secretly hoping he would say, "Let's go gamble." When he did, which was most of the time, she would appear to acquiesce for his sake. Leonard, on the other hand, convinced himself that he was merely trying to please Helen.

Once in recovery they each acknowledged that it was they who wanted to gamble, but used the other as an excuse. In the case of Helen and Leonard, the lie was more to themselves than to the other. At that point in time, they believed their own lies.

The folie a deux of Helen and Leonard allowed them to perpetuate their addiction until their families were forced to intervene. By this time, they had lost their home and life savings.

Recovery for Helen and Leonard involved each of them taking responsibility for their own actions. Neither could blame the other, so as they shared in their responsibility, they shared their recovery. The couple attends a support meeting together on a weekly basis. They can easily identify the pattern of self-deception and support each other in their system of checks and balances.

Often family members develop a pattern of lies to protect their finances from the gambler. Money may be hidden from the gambler in order to pay bills. Spouses may intercept tax return checks or other income. Family members become conspirators in deception, keeping money from Dad, or going through his pockets while he's asleep to determine how much he lost or if he has been gambling. The gambler's lies become the family's lies.

The gambler's biggest lie, however, is to himself. The gambler convinces himself that the more he loses, the higher the probability that he will win. The gambler always believes that he can beat the odds, whether by luck or skill.

If I flip a coin, it is as likely that it will land on heads, as it is that it will land on tails. If I flip the coin 17 times, each flip has the same odds. The gambler, however, convinces himself that if he wears his lucky hat, or if he flips the coin often enough, he will increase his chances of winning.

Mike convinced himself that, by winning back the money he lost, he would redeem himself in the eyes of Susan. Jack had a daughter that he had never met. He lived with the belief that one day he would win enough money to buy her everything she wanted, then he would go to her, declare himself her father, and everything would be perfect.

Both Mike and Jack, like most gamblers, live in a world of delusion and fantasy. They convince themselves that there is magic in their gambling and the magic will make everything beautiful. Only by facing their own lies can they begin to recover.

In the long run, honesty will take some practice on the part of both partners, and some assistance from the counselor. On an individual level, the counselor will need to reinforce consistently the value of honesty to the marriage. In addition, a non-judgmental approach must be exercised in order to make it possible for the gambler to express himself honestly. It is necessary that occasional lapses be met with understanding (not to be confused with acceptance).

The gambler will need to learn to trust his spouse not to attack him when he admits to a weakness in judgment or behavior. A cavalier attitude is not suggested, however. The lapses are serious, but are to be addressed in a problem solving, not accusative manner.

Learning to share our thoughts and fears brings all of us closer. The gambler has learned to cover up weaknesses. By sharing both hopes and fears and discussing weaknesses without fear, spouses can become best friends.

Sex is frequently a problem with the recovering couple. In some cases, sex has suffered for a long time. Gamblers may either be too depressed over losses to feel sexual, or they sublimate their sex drives with gambling action. Some gamblers are sexual only when they win. Spouses often report that sex is sporadic or non-existent.

Spouses frequently experience a reduction of sexual feelings toward the gambler after discovering the betrayal. Sexual desire can be inhibited by fatigue, depression, or anxiety. It is also frequently inhibited by repressed anger. It is difficult to feel warm and sexual toward someone you would like to strangle. Many spouses find that sexual feelings return when they begin to express their feelings of anger, and when they begin to feel safer through self-empowerment. The use of a journal, coupled with regular communication sessions, can assist in the former.

Anger is frequently doled out in displaced, jabs of sarcasm at inappropriate moments. It is better to engage in several sessions of open hostility and clearing the air, preferably in the presence of a therapist. The gambler, at some point, will need to feel that he can get on with his life without carrying the cross for ever. Therefore, there needs to be some rule about the intermittent sarcasm. Occasional slips of indirect hostility by the spouse should be discussed in therapy sessions in a problem-solving manner.

I do not suggest, however, that feelings of fear and anxiety should not be confronted honestly. When the non-gambling spouse experiences insecurity due to some action on the part of the gambler which may be perceived as an indicator of relapse, that fear must be addressed directly by asking: "When you did so and so, I felt afraid that it meant...." The gambler must then explain his actions. If the spouse is not satisfied with the explanation, the issue is taken into the therapy session.

Susan became comfortable confronting Mike with her fears and anxieties, but only in the therapy session. Being a normally articulate and assertive individual, she continued to have difficulty acknowledging any negative feelings to Mike outside of therapy. Mike fed into her hesitancy by looking hurt whenever Susan did confront his behavior. He would respond by hanging his head and saying, "You are right." Unfortunately, this statement served to end the discussion. Susan, however, wanted and needed an explanation of what was going on inside of Mike's head.

The spouse requires and deserves a sincere apology. At some point in time, the gambler must look at his spouse and say to her, "I am so terribly sorry for what I have put you through."

Often the gambler thinks he has apologized, but he may have never actually said the words, or said them with the sincerity necessary to be believed on a deep emotional level.

Spouses often find that they do not know what to do with all of their spare time. For years, they spent time alone while one spouse was out gambling, or spent time together while one spouse was gambling. Now they find that they are together with nothing to do.

Couples will need to begin to explore new activities and interests. What did they do when they were first together (unless gambling was always a part of their lives)? They may wish to rediscover some old passions, or to develop new ones. Take a class together, learn a new skill, and join a new church group. Share fantasies about what you always wanted to do but never did. Make a wish list that does not include spending money.

Masters and Johnson's sensate focus exercises may fulfill both the sexual and time needs. These exercises involve exploring each other's erogenous zones through a sensual massage. Taking turns, each partner provides gentle, sensual strokes to all areas of the body, excluding the traditionally sexual ones at first. The idea is to discover erogenous areas that you never knew existed, or areas that have been neglected.

In sum, intimacy involves an honest communication of thoughts, ideas and feelings, a sharing of time and activities, and a genuine sensual understanding of each other's bodies and minds.

While many spouses leave their gambler, those who remain together and gambling free often find that their relationship becomes stronger than they could have ever imagined. They have fought a battle together and they have won. What a victory!

Legal and Financial Issues

As with any other illness, gambling affects all kinds of people. For many, the guilt and shame is heightened by a history of moral and ethical behavior. These individuals are shocked to find themselves engaging in deceptive, sometimes illegal, activities. Basically, they are caring, honest, responsible people.

Judy worked hard all her life as a bookkeeper. She also raised two children and took care of her home and husband. When, in her forties, her husband divorced her and her adult children moved to another state, Judy found herself feeling very lonely and depressed. One weekend, a friend took her with him to Atlantic City. The atmosphere of the casinos instantly lifted her spirits. Most important, however, Judy discovered slot machines. She found that, while focusing on the spinning fruit and listening to the music and tinkling of coins, she wasn't lonely or unhappy.

A slots casino had recently opened up near her home. She soon found herself going there after work each evening and all day on weekends. Sometimes she won, but often she lost. She exhausted all of her available funds and ran her credit cards up to the limit. She desperately searched for ways to obtain money to continue her daily visits to the slots.

One evening as she was leaving work, she wrote out a check to herself on the company account. She was sure she would be able to pay it back before the end of the week. As it turned out, she won and did cover the check. A few weeks later, however, she did it again. Only this time she wasn't so fortunate. She lost. In a panic, she wrote another check. After awhile, the check writing became easier. She was able to adjust the books accordingly and no one was the wiser. The behavior continued for nearly a year, and eventually amounted to over $100,000.

One bright sunny morning, following a good weekend at the casino, she bounced into work preparing to replenish some of the money she'd taken. An outside team of auditors was reviewing the books. Shortly after that, Judy was arrested. She faced a long prison sentence if convicted.

Having no money for an attorney, she was forced to seek the help of a public defender. Fortunately for Judy, the public defender had been educated on gambling related crimes and established a diminished capacity defense.

Diminished capacity is when an individual knows something is wrong, but lacks the ability to control the behavior. Gambling addiction can, under the right circumstances, be used as diminished capacity, or a mitigating circumstance. Judy was given probation and ordered to pay restitution.

Not all gamblers who commit illegal acts are innocent victims of their own addiction, however. Gambling is a natural magnet for the unscrupulous and character disordered. In particular, narcissistic and anti-social personality disorders are found in a high proportion of gamblers. A description of these disorders is found in Part III. The anti-social or narcissistic personality disorder in combination with a gambling addiction can create a dangerous synergy. It is these individuals who are most likely to become cons. Let those who enter their circle of influence beware. They are potential victims. While a gambler, in the desperation phase of the addiction, may engage in fraudulent activities, for the con fraud is a way of life. He moves from victim to victim, funding his gambling activities without remorse. Setting up the con becomes part of the excitement and action, equal to and part of the gambling action itself. While the goal of the con is usually money, it is the action that is most exciting.

Over all, most gamblers will tell you that their motivation for gambling has little to do with money. They gamble for the excitement, the escape. It makes them feel good. If they win, they just give the money back. The primary purpose is the action, to continue to gamble.

Nevertheless, money is the train on which the gambler rides. He requires money to gamble, and it is the need for money that can lead to unethical and illegal behaviors. It is also the depletion of money that creates devastation. Consequently, it is necessary to address the role of money as it relates to gambling and recovery.

Our attitudes toward money begin early in life. Children of gamblers experience the rush of the big win when the parent comes home laden with presents and good cheer. Life is good! The message is twofold: money is to be spent, and money is love.

One does not need to be the child of a gambler to receive that message, however. Parents who are emotionally absent may give money and gifts as a substitute for the time and energy that is focused elsewhere. Children are rewarded materially for succeeding in school. Consequently, reinforcement is superficial rather than intrinsic. The value of immediate and material gratification becomes the norm.

It is difficult for those who have never learned delayed gratification to manage money. Money is spent; there will be more. There is also little internal value placed on how money is attained. Money is, in and of itself, the goal. Money enhances our self-esteem. Money gives us satisfaction. Money IS success!

In addition to living in a society of immediate gratification and material worth, we also live in a society that perpetuates adolescence. During adolescence and extended adolescence (which often exists in the college years), we maintain the belief that someone is responsible for us. We are not responsible for our own actions. If we fall, someone will catch us. If we make a mess, someone will clean it up. Life does not appear real, but rather like an ongoing movie in which we are mere observers asking to be entertained.

This is not to say that those of us who are good money managers are not susceptible to gambling addiction. No one is completely immune to the lure of the quick and effortless win. However, the individual who can not bear to part with more than a few hard-earned dollars is more likely to give up quickly after that initial loss. Many want something concrete to show for their money. "When I put sixty cents in a machine, I want a soda."

Therefore, the first step in money management is a major attitude adjustment:

- If you can't afford it, wait until you can.
- If the money is not in your hand (or checkbook) it does not exist.
- Always put aside some percentage (no matter how small) of whatever you earn.
- Money buys goods and services, not love or friendship.

If you want to do something nice for a friend, then bake them a cake, scrub a floor, clean their garage, or fix their car. You don't need to buy them something expensive. Birthdays and holidays are open season for running up credit card debt that we cannot afford.   Living on credit is the American way. It is also the way to short-term ruin. Credit cards are fine for identification and emergencies. They can also be used as a way to take advantage of sales or bargains so long as you can pay off the card at the end of the month. Interest rates are more expensive than we realize.

Most of us, however, use those cards as a vehicle for obtaining immediate gratification. Life is short. We want it all now. Then, we find ourselves overwhelmed by debt for something we have already enjoyed, used, eaten, or broken.

While this may sound like depression economics, for the potential gambler (and certainly for the addicted gambler) these attitude changes are critical to his survival. Learning to appreciate money by budgeting, managing, and saving are the first steps to financial redemption.

The gambler who has dug him so deeply in the financial hole that he feels he can never recover will often chase those losses, yearning for a big win to save the day. Unfortunately, the hole just gets deeper. This is when you cut your losses and begin the 3-step restructuring process.

1.   Ask someone to take over your money. To the gambler's chagrin, this means confessing to the level of debt and the depth of the problem. At this point in time, however, you are too far out of control. Someone must take over. This could be your spouse, a family member, or a consumer

credit counseling bureau. Turn all your credit cards, checking, savings, and other accounts over to this individual.

2.   Begin the process of determining what you owe and to whom. Write letters to all of your creditors, telling them that you have a gambling problem and asking for a payment schedule.

3.   Sit down with your family and money manager and work out a budget. Include everything you owe, including restitution. Arrange to be given just enough cash to continue working or looking for work. This is the hardest part, because it may appear that it will take years to get out of debt. There is no quick fix.

Restitution involves paying back money taken, borrowed, or stolen from family and friends. While it may not be immediately seen as part of the debt, it is equally important. This includes jewelry and articles pawned or sold, education or retirement funds tapped, and insurance policies borrowed against. Restitution is a vital part of the gambler's recovery, and it is necessary that it be included in the debt process.

Loved ones need to understand that it is necessary that they not bail out the gambler. A bail out is when the friend or family member provides a loan large enough to clean up the debt. Bankruptcy is often seen as a bail out. The reason the bail out does not work is that it takes the responsibility away from the gambler. He continues to believe that a quick fix is the solution. Once the problem is taken care of, it is business as usual.

Spouses and close family members must adhere to the money control without flexibility. This is often difficult. You want to trust your loved one; you want him to be happy. He has been so good for so long. So why not let him have the MAC or Visa card? This is like offering just one cigarette to one who has quit smoking. Why test fate?

Martha took over the finances for her son, Jeff, who had moved back home. Jeff had run up heavy gambling debts with poker buddies. The games began in college as a form of entertainment. Eventually, the friends invited other, more experienced players. The losses were heavy. Jeff was unable to pay, and the older gamblers became threatening.

Martha feared for her son and bailed him out. At the same time, however, she insisted that Jeff go to Gambler's Anonymous, and she began to attend Gamanon. At their urging, she took over Jeff's finances.

Jeff was forced to quit school and obtain a job. He had his check directly deposited into his mother's account. She gave Jeff just enough money to pay for gas and lunches.

This worked for about two months. Then, Jeff began to urge Martha to give him control of his finances again. He needed to feel responsible, he pleaded. Jeff worked on Martha day and night until she gave in. Within two weeks, Jeff was deeper in debt.

This time, Jeff's stepfather took over and refused to allow Jeff back into the home. Jeff began cashing bad checks and was eventually incarcerated.

For the individual who perceives money as success, finding himself on a fixed income, with little disposable cash is tantamount to disgrace. He can no longer buy rounds or pick up dinner checks. Holidays and birthdays are particularly painful.

Jane and Alex had survived their first year after Alex's gambling had nearly cost them their home. They had worked out a budget and estimated that it would take them five years to get out of debt. In the interim, there would be no frills.

Their first Christmas, Jane found herself feeling angry and resentful. Alex was sullen and defensive. They bickered constantly over everything, except for the real subject. Both Jane and Alex loved big holidays with lots of presents. Alex always put expensive jewelry in Jane's stocking, and the couple bought gifts for their families. This year, Jane and Alex had to tell their families there would be no gifts. Jane looked toward Christmas morning like a cold. icy rain. She was feeling unloved, and Alex was feeling guilty and humiliated. Their sex life had become nonexistent.

In the midst of one of their many arguments, the couple finally acknowledged their feelings about the holidays. Jane realized that Alex felt even worse because he could not give her the glamorous gifts of the past. After a tearful reconciliation, they began to talk about how they could get through the holidays. They began to brainstorm about alternative forms of gifts. Jane loved foot rubs. Alex wanted Jane to dress up provocatively for him alone.

They made up little gift certificates, wrapping them in colorful paper, and put them in their stockings. They did the same for family members, offering to cook a meal for one, clean the garage for another. The certificates were wrapped in boxes.

The gifts were such a success that the family agreed to continue the process. Family members were asked to write a list of things they wanted done, but never felt like doing. Jane and Alex enhanced their sex lives with little erotic services, often taken for granted and forgotten. Alex wrote the lyrics to a song and had his brother put it to music. Another family member recorded it, and he gave it to Jane for her birthday. No piece of jewelry could ever have been more appreciated.

Some of us can remember when gifts were homemade, food, clothing, household objects, art, etc. These gifts always embodied a lot of love and time. Over the years, such forms of gift giving converted to gift buying which seemed to require larger and larger sums of money. People replaced time and love with money.

In summary, we need to re-evaluate our attitude toward money and what it symbolizes. We need to determine our self worth in deeper, more meaningful ways. The significance should be in what we have given of ourselves to another person, not what have we bought for them.

Who we are is not how much we make. We must make a connection to a value system that goes beyond the superficial. Most of all, we need to take each day and make it meaningful to us and to those around us. Learning the art of patience enhances appreciation of that for which we have waited, saved, and worked. This we must teach our children, now. Tell them you love them for who they are, not for their grades in school, or social achievements, or sports scores, but for them alone. Don't buy them things. Spend time with them!

Part V

HOW? Treatment issues

Part five will address issues of treatment, including assessments, support groups, counseling, medication, and the coaching approach.

Treatment overview

Pathological gambling was first included in the DSM-III (Diagnostic and Statistical Manual, third edition) in 1980. The first tool that was widely used to diagnose this disorder was the SOGS (South Oaks Gambling Screen (Lesieur and Blume, 1987). It is a 20-item scale that includes items related to time spent, money gambled, arguments, and borrowing. The instrument fell under criticism, however, as gambling prevalence increased across socio-economic groups. Many items were not found to be relevant to all groups.

A new instrument was developed based on the revised DSM-IV criteria. The NODS refers to the NORC (National Opinion Research Center at the University of Chicago) DSM Screen for Gambling Problems. The NODS includes 17 lifetime items and 17 corresponding past-year items relating to the criteria established for pathological gambling in the DSM-IV. The NODs has replaced the SOGs among most treatment provider groups.

In addition to the gambling assessment, many treatment providers also evaluate overall addictive behaviors through the use of such instruments as the Addiction Severity Index. This instrument evaluates level of severity for substances such as drugs and alcohol as well as gambling and mental illness. The assessment also looks at personal and family history, including relationships, mental illness, former drug or alcohol use by family members, and legal and financial issues.

Additional pieces of the individual picture may be obtained through the use of SCID (Structured Clinical Interview of DSM) I and II. Axis I, or mental health diagnoses may be obtained from the SCID-I, while personality disorders are indicated through the SCID-II.

In many cases, the above tools are used by Human Resources as a method of identifying potential problems. Mental health agencies and practitioners may screen clients who present with depression and anxiety. Finally, the criminal justice system has begun to have clients screened when a crime involving money has been committed by someone without a prior criminal history.

Practitioners generally agree that there are two questions which, if answered positively, will identify a gambling problem: Do you ever lie about the amount of time or money you spend gambling? Do you ever return the next day after gambling to recover your losses?

Unfortunately, treatment usually results only after a problem has become serious enough to warrant attention. As cold remedies vary, so does treatment for gambling addiction. Many will tell you that there is only one treatment that works but, as with diets, we have to find the one that works for us. Sometimes a combination of treatment techniques is most effective. Some of the techniques that have been used satisfactorily include:

- Helpline
- Support groups
- In-patient treatment
- Intensive outpatient treatment
- Outpatient counseling/Medication
- Coaching

Helpline. Most states have a gambling helpline number. This is usually an 800 number that can be accessed 24 hours a day. Sometimes, there is a general number that deals with all mental health and addictions problems. Helpline or crisis numbers are listed in the front of the phone book in your area. Helplines are usually staffed by volunteers. The purpose of the helpline call is to obtain information and to make a connection to professional or specialized assistance. If the caller is in life threatening crisis, the volunteer will probably initiate steps to reduce risk. These steps could include a call to 911 or to a crisis intervention service.

Some gamblers will call the helpline only when they have reached a point of desperation and see no way out. The helpline volunteers will listen to you and attempt to reassure you that there is help available. When you are in agreement, they will give you the necessary information to obtain the help you need. In some cases, the caller just needs to talk without fear of retribution.

The call is confidential, with the exception that when a caller indicates that he may harm himself, or someone else, the volunteer is required to initiate steps to ensure safety, including a call to 911. The caller may then be subject to possible hospitalization or psychiatric screening.

Support Groups. The number one support group for gamblers is Gambler's Anonymous (GA). GA operates through a 12-step program very much like Alcoholics Anonymous. Gambler's Anonymous is described in detail in the next chapter.

In-patient treatment. In-patient treatment or hospitalization, may be beneficial for those who find themselves unable to withdraw without supervision and/or medication. Hospitalization may also be beneficial for those who are suffering from severe depression. Such treatment is limited to those who can either afford to pay or for whom insurance will cover gambling treatment.

Treatment for gambling addiction, while listed as a diagnosis in the DSM-IV, is still not covered under many insurance plans. If the individual is depressed or anxious, treatment may be covered under one of those diagnoses.

Intensive out-patient treatment. One alternative to hospitalization is intensive out-patient treatment. The individual will attend a daily program, several days per week, for several weeks. Treatment is a combination of individual and group counseling, and may also involve family counseling. Often, medication is administered. After the intensive program, an aftercare plan is developed that usually involves continued counseling and/or support group participation. These programs are also usually limited to those who can afford them or for whom insurance plans will cover the treatment.

Outpatient counseling. Outpatient counseling may be combined with a support group or with medication as a preferred treatment. Some counselors work with psychiatrists who prescribe the medication. Or, the individual may get medication from the family physician at the recommendation of the counselor. Outpatient counseling is described in detail in the chapter entitled *Counseling and Medication.*

Coaching. Often referred to as Life Coaching or Coaching through Recovery, coaching is an alternative to counseling that focuses more on goal attainment than insight. A thorough description of coaching techniques and approaches can be found in the Coaching chapter.

If you think you have a gambling problem, or you know someone who does, you may get help by calling the local helpline number. The appendix lists the numbers of Gambling Councils for the various states. If your state is not listed, any of the neighboring state councils will provide information on how to obtain assistance in your area.

Support Groups

The most widely used and best-known support group for gamblers is Gambler's Anonymous (GA). The first meeting of GA was held on Friday, September 13, 1957, in Los Angeles, California. The organization sprang out of a meeting between two men who were battling an obsession for gambling. The two began to meet regularly and found that the meetings helped them to maintain their abstinence to gambling. They determined from their meetings that they needed to bring about certain character changes within themselves in order to prevent relapses from occurring. They used as a guide the spiritual principles, which had been so successful for other addictions.

Consequently, GA operates through a 12-step program, which is very much like Alcoholics Anonymous. For the purpose of anonymity, members use only their first names and last initial. The members of the group are all gamblers in recovery. They are encouraged to confront their addiction to gambling, and the irrational belief process associated with it, in a supportive environment. They work through their 12-step recovery program, usually focusing on one step each week. The group uses weekly readings and encourages mentoring of other gamblers. The philosophy is complete abstinence. The belief is acceptance of powerlessness over the addiction. The foundation is spiritual, acceptance of a higher power, although the individual determines the concept of a higher power, and no particular religious affiliation is encouraged.

The concept of spirituality is used to describe characteristics of the human mind that represent the highest and finest qualities. These qualities include kindness, generosity, honesty, and humility. They believe it is important that they carry the message of hope to other compulsive gamblers.

After 30 days, GA will provide debt relief counseling during which the member can get assistance in working out a plan of restitution to pay back bills. The members will schedule a meeting with the family and develop a list of all debts, including money borrowed from the family. Letters will be written to the debtors asking for an acceptable payment plan. Sometimes interest will be reduced or forgiven. Then a reasonable payment plan is developed.

GA views bankruptcy as a bailout. It is important that the gambler take responsibility for his gambling debts as part of his recovery. Some GA groups also consider consumer credit counseling to be a bailout. As with bankruptcy, consumer credit counseling services may have a detrimental impact on your credit rating.

Even though the concept of a higher power can be interpreted individually, many are put off by the spiritual component of GA. Others find that the rule of total abstinence is too constrictive. GA considers all gambling; even an occasional lottery ticket or scratch off from soda cans, to be unacceptable.

Women have complained that many GA meetings are male dominated and overpowering. As more and more women are developing gambling problems, however, the numbers of female members at the GA meetings are growing. Women find that they can shop around until they find a particular meeting that has a higher percentage of female participants.

One solution to the GA dilemma has been to develop other non-GA support groups, particularly women's groups. These groups do not necessarily focus on a higher power and are less restrictive. The goal is sharing feelings and providing support.

Many feel that the support and camaraderie of the support groups are very helpful. Some members continue for years and develop close friendships. We need to remember, however, that support groups are comprised of recovering addicts. They are not professional counselors. There is no professional facilitator. At times, the groups may become too intense or confrontational for some individuals. Others feel that the members are too free with advice. The combination of the support group and counseling, however, can provide a beneficial balance.

The 12-steps of GA are as follows:

1. We admitted we were powerless over gambling—that our lives had become unmanageable.
2. Came to believe that a Power greater than ourselves could restore us to a normal way of thinking and living.
3. Made a decision to turn our will and our lives over to the care of this Power of our own understanding.
4. Made a searching and fearless moral and financial inventory of ourselves.
5. Admitted to ourselves and to another human being the exact nature of our wrongs.
6. Were entirely ready to have these defects of character removed.
7. Humbly asked God (of our understanding) to remove our shortcomings.
8. Made a list of all persons we had harmed and became willing to make amends to them all.
9. Made direct amends to such people wherever possible, except when to do so would injure them or others.
10. Continued to take personal inventory and when we were wrong, promptly admitted it.
11. Sought through prayer and meditation to improve our conscious contact with God as we understood Him, praying only for knowledge of His will for us and the power to carry that out.
12. Having made an effort to practice these principles in all our affairs, we tried to carry this message to other compulsive gamblers.

Gambler's Anonymous (1984, 1991, 1998)

Counseling and Medication

Before entering into a discussion about counseling for problem gamblers, we first need to examine the issue of abstinence vs. harm reduction. Abstinence is clearly the approach of GA, and is also the philosophy of most addiction counselors. However, with the increasing drop-out rate, professionals are examining the concept of harm reduction.

Harm reduction involves the practice of cutting back on the addiction or activity in order to reduce the harm it is causing in ones life. For example, an individual who drinks two six-packs a night is at risk of having an automobile accident. However, if he reduces his drinking to one or two beers he is more likely to drive safely.

A gambler who is spending all of his money and time at the casino might cut back to one or two nights a week. He may take a limited amount of money, leaving his credit cards and checkbook at home. Proponents of this method state that if the harm is reduced, then gambling his no longer a problem.

If, however, we believe that brain chemistry is altered by gambling activity, and that if addicted to a substance or action we perpetuate the addiction by continuing the habit, then even a small amount of time at the casino is putting the individual at risk. Smoking cessation groups often use the term: *you are only a puff away from a pack a day.*

From a counseling perspective, however, we can approach the issue through the use of a motivational interviewing technique. While we may believe that abstinence is truly the treatment of choice, we do not wish to lose our client by insisting that he can never buy so much as a lottery ticket. Consequently, we refrain from any such declaration and work with the client on his specific level of readiness. This particular approach

(Miller and Rollnick (1991) and Prochaska and DiClemente (1986) is much more supportive than the traditional confrontational approach, and works with the gambler to provide insight and information and then assistance in the change process when readiness occurs.

Outpatient counseling may be combined with a support group or with medication as a preferred treatment. Some counselors work with psychiatrists who prescribe the medication or the individual may get medication from the family physician at the recommendation of the counselor.

Some of the medications which have proved effective in the treatment of gambling problems include: Prozac, Anafranil, Luvox, and Wellbutrin. Prozac and Luvox are serotonin re-uptake inhibitors. They impact on the neurotransmitter serotonin. The medication inhibits the reuptake of serotonin in the synapse, and thereby, increasing the amount remaining. Serotonin provides a sense of well-being. Wellbutrin has proved successful in the treatment of ADHD.

Naltrexone, which has been used very effectively in substance abuse, is being tried with some gamblers (Crockford, 1998). The way that Naltrexone works is to reduce the craving by acting as an opiod antagonist. The addictive substance (or activity) no longer provides the same level of pleasure; therefore, the craving lessens. The results of Naltrexone for treatment of pathological gambling are not yet conclusive, but research on its use continues.

It is important to consult a counselor who is trained in the treatment of gambling addiction. Many counselors assume that treating gamblers is no different from other addictions, but there is extensive training provided in gambling treatment. Helplines and Gambling Councils provide lists of counselors who are certified to provide such treatment.

Outpatient counseling usually addresses financial controls. Developing a money management system is frequently a priority in the treatment process. A plan is developed for restitution of debts. Control of money is almost always assigned to another individual. The counselor meets with the client and money manager together.

In addition to money management, much of counseling with gamblers involves a focus toward a reality-based orientation as opposed to the world of fantasy. Cognitive-behavioral techniques are often used to retrain the gambler's thinking process and develop new behavioral patterns.

Cognitive therapy is designed to restructure a distorted thought system. One of the major erroneous beliefs of the gambler is that he has some control over the outcome of gambling, and unrealistic expectations of winning. Some of the restructuring involves teaching the gambler to understand and accept the concept of randomness and to identify faulty perceptions of reality, such as the need to be perfect, or that success equals money (Beck, 1979).

Behavioral exercises are frequently included in an effort to teach the gambler better ways to cope with stress and frustration. Many gamblers develop a sense of learned helplessness, a feeling that they have no way to cope other than to escape through gambling. Behavioral techniques teach delaying tactics to slow down the impulsive move toward gambling as a coping mechanism and alternative strategies.

Many gamblers have never developed a sense of trust, or the ability to accept themselves or others realistically. Gambling has become a means to prove worthiness and to overcome fears of abandonment and rejection. The counselor provides a safe haven where the gambler can develop a sense of trust as he learns to integrate the good and bad aspects of himself.

The family or spouse may become involved in the counseling process. Many gamblers have lost their support system. Family and friends have given up. If a relationship can be salvaged, effort is made to work with that individual, or group of individuals. Communication and conflict management skills are critical to the survival of the relationship.

Some gambling counselors include spirituality counseling (often referred to as pastoral counseling) in their treatment process. Many counselors believe that an absence of a spiritual connection can create a drive toward artificial stimulation in an attempt to fill the void.

Some insurance companies will pay for outpatient treatment, many will not. Many states are providing funds for the treatment of gambling problems. This information can be provided by the helpline or by the gambling council in your state.

The rule of thumb in seeking a counselor is to try out your counselors as you would your running shoes. If they feel right, then work with them. If not, try another pair. Counselors are individuals. Some may be compatible with your personality and needs. Some may not. It is critical that you verify their credentials. Ask for proof of their academic degrees and certifications. Ask if they are affiliated with a nationally approved gambling council.

Strategic Coaching through Recovery

Anyone who has ever gone on a diet knows that the real struggle comes after the weight has been lost. We can all overcome our temptations for a brief time. We can, with help, stop our self-destructive behaviors.

When a gambler has stopped gambling, reduced the chaos in his life, and restored his relationships, that is when he is at risk for relapse. He may believe that he is now in control of his life, and is tempted to test the waters to see just how strong he is.

A technique called coaching through recovery is a goal-oriented approach to changing ones life. The program includes a values identification process to assist in taking control of ones life and reducing the risk of relapse. The first step in the process is to identify the dark spot.

Most of us have a dark spot, a seed of fear or insecurity within us that activates our need to run in desperation. We cannot heal our dark spot without first coming face- to-face with it. It may be a fear of failure, or we may be terrified of abandonment. We may feel empty inside, while smiling outwardly. We may engage in inappropriate relationships that damage our self-esteem and well-being rather than face life alone.

We may learn to cope with our dysfunctional existence by self-medicating our pain with food, drugs (legal or illegal), alcohol, sex, spending, or gambling. With support and encouragement, we may discontinue our destructive forms of self-medication—temporarily. However, if the dark spot is not identified, the fear and anxiety will ultimately return. The old habits will also return, or may be replaced by another habit.

Once the dark spot is identified, the coaching process begins with the setting of a life goal. What would it take to banish the spot once and for all? The concept behind coaching, then, is to identify those dark spots, and then to banish them forever by strengthening our confidence and learning to set realistic and manageable goals.

For example, fear of aloneness is often fear of ourselves. Yet, in order to develop true intimacy with another, we must first develop love for ourselves, embracing our aloneness.

Gloria gambled to assuage her unhappy home life. Her husband was cold and verbally abusive. Yet, she felt she could not survive without him on a financial level. Her goal became to finish her degree and get a job.

Jenny's problem was more complex. She remained in a loveless relationship in spite of the fact that she was not only the primary breadwinner, but also managed the household. Her father had abandoned her during her adolescence, and the thought of ending her relationship stimulated memories of the pain and anger she'd felt over the loss of her father. Her goal was two-fold. First, she needed to come to terms with her emotions, sadness and anger, related to her father.

She wrote him a long letter explaining her feelings and also spoke at length with her mother. She discovered that her father had not, in fact, chosen to abandon her, but that her mother had been so angry over the divorce that she'd refused to allow him to see his daughter. He felt that pursuing contact would create conflict for her and cause her pain. Her mother, now in a happy marriage and realizing the pain her daughter suffered, confessed her weakness. Consequently, father and daughter began an attempt to develop a new relationship.

Jenny's second goal was to enjoy spending time alone. She ultimately ended her marriage, and instead of filling her lonely hours with gambling, she began learning about herself, her likes and dislikes. She took a music appreciation class and spent long hours listening to CDs.

Not all goals are easy to achieve; many have obstacles. Many require personal changes in order to reach the goal. The coach acts as a guide to identify the steps toward recovery. Sometimes smaller, sub-goals must be identified and met prior to attempting the larger goal.

Does this mean that we will never feel anxious or sad? Of course, not. It does, however, mean that we will be able to cope with our disappointments and setbacks without turning to our old negative habits.

In review, the coaching process is in two parts. The first part involves the identification of the dark spot. This may be done is as little as one session, or it may takes several. Once the dark spot has been identified, we move into the 12-session goal achievement process.

The 12-week process begins with the identification of a goal, works through the barriers that have been encountered in the past and methods to overcome them. Specific supports are identified as well as self-help techniques. These may include spiritual or personal support, and self-motivation exercises.

Finally, when success has been achieved, we identify our method for continuing the process and maintaining control over our lives.

Coaches may work with clients from a strictly coaching perspective, or may combine coaching with counseling techniques. A list of certified coaches may be obtained through professional organizations, such as the International Coaching Federation, or through professional counseling organizations such as the American Counselors Association or the National Board of Certified Counselors.

Again, anytime you seek out a counselor or a coach, verify their credentials. You have a right to see their licenses, degrees, and certifications. If they are not clearly displayed, asked to see them.

APPENDIX

LIST OF GAMBLING COUNCILS

NATIONAL COUNCIL ON PROBLEM GAMBLING, INC.
208 G Street, NW
Washington, D.C. 20002
(202)547-9204

*Affiliate Councils**

Arizona Council on Compulsive Gambling, Inc.
P.O. Box 23896
Phoenix, AZ 85063
(602)212-0278
800-777-7207 Hotline

California Council on Problem Gambling, Inc.
121 S. Palm Canyon Drive, Ste. 207
Palm Springs, CA 92262
(760) 320-0234
800-322-8748 (CA only)

Canadian Foundation on Compulsive Gambling (Ontario)
505 Consumers Rd., Ste 605
Willowdale, Ont. M2J4V8 Canada
(416)499-9800 (day)
(416)222-7477(evening)
888-391-1111 nationwide

Colorado Council on Compulsive Gambling, Inc.
P.O. Box 280265
Lakewood, CO 80228-0265
(303)220-1911, Ext 4

Connecticut Council on Compulsive Gambling, Inc.
47 Clapboard Hill Rd, Ste 6
Guildford, CT 06437
(203)453-0138
888-789-7777

Delaware Council on Gambling Problems, Inc.
100 West 10th Street, Ste 303
Wilmington, DE 19801-1677
(302)655-3261
888-850-8888

Florida Council on Compulsive Gambling, Inc.
P.O. Box 3487
Longwood, FL 32779-0487
(407) 865-6200
800-426-7711 nationwide

Georgia Council on Compulsive Gambling
2300 Peachford Rd. Ste. 1111
Atlanta, GA 30338
(770)242-8781
(770)986-9510

Illinois Council on Problem and Compulsive Gambling, Inc.
P.O. Box 6489
Evanston, Il 60204

(847)296-2026
800-426-2546 nationwide

Indiana Council on Problem Gambling
10104 Manhattan Circle
FT. Wayne, IN 46825
(219)489-0506

Iowa Problem Gambling Council, Inc.
1544 2nd Ave.
Des Moines, IA 50314
(515)282-7322
800-238-7633 (IA only)

Kentucky Council on Compulsive Gambling
2407 Willowbrook Ct.
Prospect, KY 40059
(502) 629-8868

Louisiana Association on Compulsive Gambling
820 Jordan St., Ste 415
Shreveport, LA 71101-4581
(318)222-7657

Maryland Council on Compulsive Gambling, Inc.
503 Maryland Avenue
Baltimore, MD 21228
(410)788-8599

Massachusetts Council on Compulsive Gambling, Inc.
190 High St., Ste 6

Boston, MA 02110
(617)426-4554
800-426-1234 nationwide

Michigan Council on Problem Gambling
1035 St. Antoine street, Ste 103
Detroit, MI 48226
(313)256-9316
800-270-7117 (MI only)

Mississippi Council on Compulsive Gambling, Inc.
1900 N. West Street, Ste. D
Jackson, MS 39202-1784
(601)353-4010
888-777-9696

Missouri Council on Problem Gambling Concerns, Inc.
5128 Brookside Blvd.
Kansas City, MO 64112-2736
(816)889-4662

Nebraska Council on Compulsive Gambling
703 West 24 Avenue
Bellevue, NE 68005
(402)291-0980
800-560-2126 nationwide

Nevada Council on Problem Gambling, Inc.
3006 S. Maryland Pkwy.,Ste. 405
Las Vegas, NV 89109
(702)369-9740
800-522-4700

New Hampshire Council on Problem Gambling, Inc.
P.O. Box 13
west Chesterfield, NH 03466
(603)256-6262

Council on Compulsive Gambling of New Jersey, Inc.
1315 W. State Street
Trenton, NJ 08618
(609)599-3299
800-426-2537 nationwide

New York Council on Problem Gambling, Inc.
The Dodge Building
119 Washington Avenue
Albany, NY 12210-2292
(518)427-1622
800-437-1611 (NY only)

Council on Compulsive and Problem Gambling of North Dakota, Inc.
P.O. Box 7362
Bismarck, ND 58507-7362
(701)255-3692
800-472-2911 (ND only)

Ohio Council on Problem Gambling
P.O. Box 770908
Lakewood, OH 44107
(216)808-9877
888-869-9600 (OH only)

Oregon Problem Gambling Program
Assoc. of Oregon Community Mental Health Program

Committee GAT Clinical Division
1201 Court Street, NE
P.O. Box 866
Salem, OR 97308
(503)320-9654/(503)872-0156

Council on Compulsive Gambling of Pennsylvania
1002 Longspur Rd.
Audubon, PA 19403
(215)744-1880
800-848-1880(PA only)

Puerto Rico compulsive Gamblers Help Program
P.O. Box 363952
San Juan, PR 00936-3952
(787)250-7999
800-981-2002 (PR only)

Rhode Island Council on Problem Gambling
P.O. Box 6551
Providence, RI 02940-6551
(401)724-8552

South Carolina Council on Problem Gambling, Inc.
1201 Main Street, Ste. 1980
Columbia, SC 29201
(803)748-1313

South Dakota Council on Problem Gambling, Inc.
3818 S. Western Avenue, Ste 177
Sioux Falls, SD 57105

(605)987-2751
888-781-4357 (SD only)

Texas Council on Problem and Compulsive Gambling, Inc.
P.O. Box 835895
Richardson, TX 75080
(972)889-2331
800-742-0443 (TX only)

Vermont Council on Problem Gambling, Inc.
P.O. Box 803
Brattleboro, VT 05302
(802)257-7785

Washington State Council on Problem Gambling
P.O. Box 55272
Seattle, WA 98155-0272
(206)546-6133
800-547-6133 (WA only)

Wisconsin Council on Problem Gambling
1825 Riverside Drive
Green Bay, WI 54301
(920)437-8888
800-426-2535 (WI only)

REFERENCES

American Psychiatric Association. (1994) *Diagnostic and Statistical Manual of Mental Disorders.*
Washington, D.C.

Bandura, A. (1986). *Social foundations of thought and action: a social-cognitive theory.* Englewood Cliffs, NJ: Prentice-Hall.

Beck, A.T., Rush, A.J., Shaw, B.F. & Emery, G. (1979) *Cognitive Therapy of Depression.* New York: The Guilford Press

Bergler, Edmund (1985). *The Psychology of Gambling.* USA: International Universities Press, Inc.

Berman, L. and Seigel, M. (1992). *Behind the 8-Ball: A Guide for Families of Gamblers.* New York: Fireside/Parkside

Birnbaum, K. (1914). Die *Psychopathischen Verbrecker, 2nd Ed.* Leipzig: Thieme.

Blaszcynski, Alex and Silove, Derrick. (Summer, 1995) Cognitive and behavior therapies for pathological gambling. *Journal of Gambling studies* 11:195-220.

Ciarrocchi, J. & Richardson, R. (1980). Profile of compulsive gamblers in treatment: update and comparisons. *Journal of Gambling Behavior,* 5(I), 53-65.

Cleckley, H. M. (1964*). The Mask of Sanity,* 4th Ed. St. Louis: C. V. Mosby.

Crockford, D.N (1998). Naltrexone in the treatment of pathological gambling and alcohol dependence. *Canadian Journal of Psychiatry,* 43(1), 86.

Custer, R. L. and Milt, H. (1985). *When Luck Runs Out: Help for Compulsive Gamblers and their Families.* New York: Warner Brothers.

Custer, R. L. & Custer, L. P. (December, 1978). *Characteristics of the recovering compulsive gambler: A survey of 150 members of Gamblers Anonymous.* Paper presented at the Fourth Annual Conference on Gambling, University of Nevada.

DeObaldia, R. & Parsons, O.A. (1984). Relationship of neuropsychological performance to primary alcoholism and self-reported symptoms of childhood minimal brain dysfunction. *Journal of Studies on Alcohol,* 45, 386-392.

Dostoevsky, Fydor (1966). *The Gambler.* Great Britain: Hazell Watson & Viney, Ltd.

Frankl, Viktor E. (1959). *Man's Search for Meaning.* New York: Simon & Schuster, Inc.

Gamblers Anonymous (1984). *Sharing Recovery Through Gamblers Anonymous.* Los Angeles: Gamblers Anonymous.

Gamblers Anonymous (1991). *What is GA?* Minn.: Hazelden Educational Materials.

Gamblers Anonymous (1998) Los Angeles: Gamblers Anonymous.

Gardner J. (March, 1986). *The relationship between conscious and unconscious processes and individual creativity.* Invited Address, California State Psychological Association Convention, san Francisco.

Harpur, Timothy J, Hart, Stephen D. and Hare, Robert D. (1994). *Personality of the psychopath. In Personality Disorders and the Five-Factor Model of Personality.* Costa, Paul T., Ed. Washington, D. C: American Psychological Association.

Heineman, Mary (1992). *Losing Your Shirt.* Center City, Minnesota: Hazeldon.

Horney, K. (1945). *Our Inner Conflicts.* New York: Norton.

Humphrey, S. H. and Walsh, J. M. (June 1998). *Assessment and Treatment of GamblingDisorders in a Community Mental Health Center.* Paper presented at the National Conference on Problem Gambling. Las Vegas, Nevada..

Jacobs, Durand F. (1998). An Overarching Theory of Addiction: A New Paradigm for Understanding and Treating Addictive Behaviors. Presented to the National Research Council, September 3, 1998.

Kernberg, O. (1975). *Borderline Conditions and Pathological Narcissism.* New York: Jason Aronson.

Krystal, H. (1982). Alexithymia and the effectiveness of psychoanalytic treatment. *International Journal of Psychoanalytic Psychotherapy* 9:353-388.

Lesieur, Henry R. (1984). *The Chase.* Rochester, VT: Schenkman Books, Inc.

Lesieur, H.R. & Blume, S.B. (1987). The South Oaks Gambling Screen (SOGS): A new instrument for the identification of pathological gamblers. *American Journal of Psychiatry,* 41, 1009-1012.

Lilienfeld, S. O. (1990). *Conceptual and empirical issues in the assesment of psychopathology.* Unpublished Manuscript.

McNeilly, D. P. & Burke, W. J. (2000). Late life gambling, the attitudes and behaviors of older adults. *Journal of Gambling Studies,* 16(4), 393-415.

Meloy, J. Reid (1988). *The Psychopathic Mind: Origins, Dynamics, and Treatment.* London: Jason Aronson, Inc.

Miller, Wm. R. & Rollnick, S. (1991). *Motivational Interviewing: Preparing People to Change Addictive Behavior.* New York: Guildford Press.

National Opinion Research Center at the University of Chicago (1999). Overview of National Survey and Community Database Research on Gambling Behavior. Presented to the National Gambling Impact Study Commission.

Pasternak, IV, A. V. & Fleming, M. F. (1999). Prevalance of gambling disorders in a primary care setting. *Archives of Family Medicine,* 8, 515-520.

Pavlov, I. (1927). *Conditioned Reflexes.* Oxford, England: University Press.

Prichard, J. C. (1835*). A Treatise on Insanity.* Trans. D. Davis. New York: Hafner.

Prochaska, J. O., & DiClemente, C. C. (1986). Toward a comprehensive model of change. In W. R. Miller & N. Heather (Eds.) *Treating Addictive Behaviors: Processes of Change*, (pp. 3-27). New York: Plenum Press.

Rugle, L. & Melamed, L. (August, 1990). *Neuropsychological assessment of attention deficit disorder in pathological gamblers.* Paper presented at the Eight International Conference on Gambling and Risk Taking, London, England.

Scannell, E. D., Quirk, M. M., smith, K., Maddern, R., & Dickerson, M. (2000). Females' coping styles and control over poker machine gambling. *Journal of Gambling Studies*, 16(4), 417-432.

Siegel, Mary Ellen and Berman, Linda (1992). *Behind the 8-Ball.* New York: Fireside/Parkside Simon and Schuster.

Skinner, B.F. (1938). *The behavior of organisms.* New York: Appleton-Century-Crofts.

*Information Provided by the National Council on Problem Gambling, Inc.

0-595-13498-X